PRISMS

Other Books by Albert Cook

PRISMS

STUDIES IN MODERN LITERATURE

by Albert Cook

1967

Indiana University Press

Bloomington & London

For

AARON ROSEN,
who has understood

Contents

Preface

WHAT ARE the philosophical bases of the literary use of language? How has modern literary practice revealed them and extended them? In contemplating these two questions, I worked my way toward this book.

As I worked, my focal considerations grew somewhat more specific than my initial philosophical questions. And my foci had a way of casting light on, and of drawing light from, related questions, "prismatically," so that each question came to require a treatment beyond the scope of one set formulation. The tendency for modern poems to present fragmentary detail could not be fully discussed in the chapter on "diffusion." That focus carried with it a further question about the sort of generality in language that would permit such fragmentation. Moreover, the thematic associativeness of the "diffuse" poem is often accompanied by a comparable principle of association in the poem's rhythms.

This further problem is touched on in the first chapter; but for adequate treatment a separate, technical chapter is needed. Another chapter, on "person," tends to open a new dimension on rhythm, as well as on "diffusion" and on "generality"; and even on modern allegory and modern dramatic action, which in turn are meant to help explain each other.

In one way, then, this book's many facets may make its organization appear scattered. It does not present a sequenced argument, historical or thematic. It does not proceed to a demonstrated conclusion. Instead it raises and, I hope, partially answers questions which in this or another form have bothered critics and theoreticians of literature. I believe these questions recommend a "prismatic" treatment. So if we ask these questions about Montale, then I feel he is

profitably discussed first as a diffuse poet, then as a poet whose statements use generality in a peculiar way, then as a practitioner who
adapts classical rhythms to an unclassical end. Consequently, instead
of getting a chapter to himself, he comes up in three separate chapters explicitly; and a fourth chapter, "Person," implicitly bears on
him. Beckett's plays are discussed as allegories in the fourth chapter,
and as exhibiting a special relation between dramatic language and
action in the fifth. A passage from Robert Lowell's *Life Studies* is
analyzed for its rhythms in the third chapter and for its presentation
of a structured self in the last. In general, I have looked repeatedly
at the same writers, and even at the same poems, when practicable,
as another way of emphasizing how one facet relates to another or
to several others.

This book rests on an assumption it only partially substantiates:
that functional categories are often also historical ones, that a way
of handling verbal material artistically not only entails a way of
seeing the world but also appears at a characteristic moment of time.
Such an assumption goes far beyond the comparable assumption underlying such historical-functional identifications as "Silver Prose,"
"Augustan Poetry," and the like. While always present, the assumption may strike the reader as especially controversial at certain points,
as in my claim that there is something quite special about the "generality" of signification in modern writing, or in my implication that
the use of recitative structures in drama becomes unmanageable in
modern times, as it was unavoidable from Aeschylus through Racine.
In the large sweep of inclusion covering the last two, indeed, my
presentation here involves a foreshortening I hope soon to redress
in a book or books about verse tragedy. In this, as in other respects,
I am no more exhaustive than a critic can be once he has slighted
one emphasis by choosing one or more others.

My choices of emphasis may puzzle the reader in two ways: they
may appear willfully deliberate, and thus unnecessarily abstract. At
the same time it may seem strange that I do not focus on works in
either of two usual ways. I do not dwell on the form of an individual

work just for its own sake, and I do not for the most part follow my own earlier practice of considering the formal implications of a genre, poetry, fiction or drama. Instead, I have found the questions I wanted to answer to be most readily classifiable around the formal conditions of making statements—hence the chapters on "generality," "allegory," and "action"; or else around the formal conditions of organizing statements—thus the chapters on "diffusion," "rhythm," and "person." Some of these conditions apply largely to a single genre; so "rhythm" and "diffusion" are confined, for my purposes, to poetry, and "action" to drama.

Of course I do not think of my two emphases as exclusive of one another: to make a statement is to begin to organize one, because all literary statements are arguably syntactic; to organize a statement in literature is also to make one. And I hope the reader will go along with me in seeing applications of one emphasis—"generality" or "diffusion,"—to some or all of the others, to "allegory" or "person," even to "rhythm" or "action." Such "prismatic" applications of one focus to another, indeed, must give my book whatever unity it may possess, as the title is meant to suggest.

I owe thanks to my students for listening to these ideas and helping me evolve them; to the Fulbright Commission for Germany, who granted me the research professorship on which I worked out the beginnings of this book, delivering a draft of the first chapter as a lecture in June, 1957, at the Freie Universität, Berlin; to the Michigan State Conference on Modern Literature for inviting me in 1963, where I discussed another chapter; to the American Philosophical Society and the Fulbright Commission for France, who gave me respectively a maintenance grant and a travel grant that allowed me to complete and enrich the book in the climate of those critics perhaps closest to it in their practise, the "structuralists"; and to the Center for Advanced Study in the Behavioral Sciences, where I put the last touches on the manuscript.

I am also grateful to my literary agent, Sterling Lord, for handling what must have seemed an odd manuscript; to Aaron Rosen, John

PRISMS

Crowe Ransom, John Hollander, Hugh Kenner, Ian Watt, Albert Hofstadter, and John Vickery, for keen suggestions; to my research assistant Stephen Rodefer, for careful work on checking details of documentation; to Dorothy Wikelund of the Indiana University Press for sensitive editing; to Eva Hesse for printing some of my Pound material in a symposium on him; and to the three places where sections of this work have appeared: the *Kenyon Review* (Spring 1959), the Michigan State *Proceedings* (1963), *College English* (October, 1966). Beyond these I am abundantly thankful to my wife Carol.

PRISMS

DIFFUSION

THE POETS we designate as most characteristically modern do not attend especially to rhetorical coherence or logical progression. Often they end with what seems at first glance a collocation of random fragments. And it is with fragments that the modern poet often begins: urgent fragments, a phrase in the head, a persistent burst of rhythm, even a quotation. If the particularity of the world has its own inscape, it may take Hopkins as long to put together a dappled thing from his notebook entries as to make the decision that poetry is permissible to the Jesuit (two versions of the same process, perhaps).

When the poem does cohere, it has been put under recognizable pressure. This is the way of Valéry and early Rilke, the poem hermetically sealed around an interpretation of a single object profoundly meditated: the severe singleness of concern gives away the violence with which the final poem has been wrested from a bewildering flux—Valéry was silent twenty years; Rilke pondered about as long over poems that dissatisfied him, until he could break forth jubilantly into a new, diffuse style.

Even the "ordered" style need not keep strictly to its object. Yeats holds to his wild swans, but in "Le Cygne" Baudelaire remembers, diffusely, a bird escaped from a cage seen once when he crossed a new bridge in Paris. He reminds himself of the inexorably changing city, the Louvre, the old Carrousel, his melancholy, and a Negress far from Africa; but first of a legendary Trojan woman (possibly— the rhythms lend this suggestion credence—filtered diffusely through Racine):

Andromaque, je pense à vous! Ce petit fleuve,
Pauvre et triste miroir où jadis resplendit
L'immense majesté de vos douleurs de veuve,
Ce Simoïs menteur qui par vos pleurs grandit,

A fécondé soudain ma mémoire fertile,
Comme je traversais le nouveau Carrousel.
Le vieux Paris n'est plus (la forme d'une ville
Change plus vite, hélas! que le coeur d'un mortel); . . .

Andromache, I think of you! This little stream,
A mirror poor and sad where once there shone
The immense majesty of your widow's sorrows,
This lying Simois that grows with your tears,

Fructified all at once my fertile memory
As I was crossing over the new Carrousel.
Old Paris is no more (a city's form
Changes more quickly, alas! than a mortal's heart);[1]

Baudelaire gets to his swan only after two more such masterfully diffuse stanzas. Consequently, the swan is not his subject, though it furnishes the title of the poem; it is not even a centrally exfoliating symbol, but merely a central point of organization for the cognitive experience attached to it. The statement happens to be as rational as one in classical poetry, but the diffusion of the poem points to an obscure relation between sights and emotions which cannot be formulated in classical terms. This attempt to express what ordinarily is inexpressible shows up in the diffusion, I believe, as much as in the tendency of recent poetry to be nonlogical, "freed from reason" as Maritain puts it, or "pure" in the terms variously applied by L'abbé Bremond and Robert Penn Warren. *Ash Wednesday* is "pure" and also "diffuse." To call its statements "pure" may serve to refine them away from the literal ("the bent goldenrod and the lost sea smell," are not just something remembered) or the simply symbolic (the Lady is not the Virgin). But the whole experience of the poem is one in which a traditional occasion for contrition becomes also a way of knowing the *world* (not just *knowing* the world), from a stair where all diversities merge. Ezekiel, Shakespeare, and the Grimms' tale of bones buried under a juniper tree, all exist not only on the same plane but also in the same even, masterly, free rhythms.

Diffusion as a mode of composition keeps faithful to the cognitive experience of which the poem is some fusion. At the beginning of the modern tradition we can recognize in poets as different as Whitman and Emily Dickinson an attempt to cope with the demands of such knowledge. Very much as Whitman's impressions are uniformly presented in the long, often disjunct, lines of his poems, the disjunctions of Emily Dickinson's impressions stand out in the punctuation of her poems, where a uniform dash is placed between the integers of poetic phrase:

> Some such Butterfly be seen
> On Brazilian Pampas—
> Just at noon—no later—Sweet—
> Then—the License closes—

> Some such Spice—express and pass—
> Subject to Your Plucking—
> As the Stars—You knew last Night—
> Foreigners—This Morning—[2]

To criticize such poems for incoherence, as Blackmur impressively does, or even to analyze them in such a way that they seem to cohere, is to overlook the essentially diffuse perceptions striving to connect a Massachusetts butterfly with a Brazilian one, "noon" with "no later" and "then," "Spice" with "express," "pass" and "Plucking," stars at night with their absence in morning. "Connect" is even too strong a word; Emily Dickinson added the word "License" as a revision for "Vision" and "Pageant." And Baudelaire's correspondences are only "échos" which "de loin se confondent." Emily Dickinson may strive to confine herself to a single experience or image, but accidentally, as it were, if not out of mistaken deference to the sort of poetic canons which Thomas Wentworth Higginson represented for her. Her stanza, with its third line rising urgently and its fourth closing definitely, tries both to allow diffusion and contain it, as her dashes preserve the unsubordinated equivalence of the perceptions. Like Whitman almost, Emily Dickinson was writing one long diffuse set of apprehensions. She sewed her manuscripts together with thread the way Whitman habitually combined his disjunct notes into longer poems. By putting his verses all in the same book with the title *Leaves of Grass,* he suggests a comparable spontaneity and equivalence for the disjunctions. Just as Emily Dickinson tends to rise so to abstractions that sometimes, particularly in her later work, whole "poems" will consist only of abstractions, so Whitman's perceptions,—initially or, as here, ultimately sensual— open cognitively into apocalypse for him:

> Swiftly arose and spread around me the peace and knowledge
>   that pass all the argument of the earth,
> And I know that the hand of God is the promise of my own,
> And I know that the spirit of God is the brother of my own,
> And that all men ever born were also my brothers, and the
>   women my sisters and lovers,
> And that a kelson of the creation is love,
> And limitless are leaves stiff or drooping in the fields,
> And brown ants in the little wells beneath them,
> And mossy scabs of the worm fence, heap'd stones, elder,
>   mullein and poke weed.[3]

In the next section Whitman leaps diffusely to another subject, then to another, as in these lines: the diffusion of statement permits an intimation of the One through the Many. A vast incorporating perception directs poetic statement to the particularities, ants in wells under leaves, mossy scabs, the very names of plants—as Hopkins found the *haecceitas* of things an indication of God. (Hopkins says in a letter to Bridges that Whitman's spirit is so close to his own he fears him.) The "spring" of Hopkins' own rhythm works to preserve the strenuousness of holding live and diverse particulars in one perception. Rhythmically, on the other hand, Whitman's line spreads, in a loose equalizing embrace of the particulars, and the last line quoted above meanders through a set of emphases where the particularities assume a spondaic, accented form: the rhythms are not structured enough to be sprung, though we pause with strong accent on the names "worm fence," "heap'd stones," "elder," "mullein," "poke weed."

Diffusion by its nature is a principle of composition, if a principle seemingly negative in that it puts the parts of a poem to some degree apart, rather than together, the expected practise not only in poems but in language generally. The poem, by virtue of being presented as a unit, pretends to some form of unity; the diffuse poem forces us to consider carefully what special unity it can have when it is composed in a way that on the surface is disunited. To ask about unity in any poem, and especially about a unity somewhat concealed by diffusion, is close to asking what a poem is finally about. The question of form raises the question of theme, and I should like to ask both questions about some diffuse poems.

To see how diffusion works, I should like to analyze in detail four poems where diffusion predominates as a method of composition: I have chosen small poems rather than such diffuse quasi-epics of our time as *Un Coup de Dés*, the *Llanto por Ignacio Sanchez Mejías*, *The Waste Land*, *The Cantos*, *Ash Wednesday*, *Paterson*, the *Duineser Elegien*, *Anabase*. And I have chosen poems whose diffusion is applied not to random particulars, but to a single occasion, a single scene, so that the content of the poem may be seen to depend the more forcibly on the diffuse procedures of rhythm and statement.

Gottfried Benn calls himself a "Hersteller der Zerrbildern"; an organizer of images that tear apart. His images are diffuse to the point of abruptness: he leaps with a jazzy, almost proud fitfulness from one to the other. In his poem "Notturno" three diffused images

set the scene, which then becomes an occasion for disjunct acidities
about human life and fate in general:

> Im Nebenzimmer die Würfel auf den Holztisch,
> benachbart ein Paar im Ansaugestadium,
> mit einem Kastanienast auf dem Klavier tritt die Natur hinzu—
> ein Milieu, das mich anspricht.
>
> Da versinken die Denkprozesse,
> die Seekrankheit, die einem tagsüber
> die Brechzentren bearbeitet,
> gehn unter in Alkohol und Nebulosem—
> endlich Daseinschwund und Seelenausglanz!
>
> Auf Wogen liegen—
> natürlich kann man untergehn,
> aber das ist eine Zeitfrage
> doch Zeit—vor Ozeanen—?
> Die waren vorher,
> vor Bewusstsein und Empfängnis,
> keiner fischte ihre Ungeheuer,
> keiner litt tiefer als drei Meter
> und das ist wenig.[4]

> In the next room the dice onto the wooden table,
> Alongside a pair in the sucking stage,
> with a chestnut branch on the piano Nature steps in—
> a milieu that appeals to me.
>
> Then sink away the thought processes,
> seasickness, which all day long
> belabors one's vertigo balance-centers,
> they go under in alcohol and the nebulous—
> finally being-fall and souls-afterglow!
>
> On waves lying—
> naturally one can go under,
> but that is a time question
> so Time—before Oceans—?
> They were before,
> before consciousness and conception,
> nobody fished their monstrosity,
> nobody suffered deeper than three meters
> and that is little.

Dice on a wooden table, a pair in the sucking stage, Nature with a chestnut branch on a piano—this farrago the poet calls a "Milieu," one that appeals to him, he says, in the sole clause of the poem where he refers directly to himself.

We may compare these dice with their possible parent, the rib statement of Mallarmé's final work *Un Coup de Dés:* "un coup de dés jamais n'abolira le hasard." A throw of dice will never abolish Chance. Benn has de-symbolized and de-generalized, so to speak, the dice of Mallarmé. His have a single throw ("auf den Holztisch," in the accusative), taking place on a definite surface, one of a concreteness underlined by the fact that it is not only a "Tisch" but a "Holztisch." But we are spared any possible glossiness in this imagery by Benn's abstention from specifying the wood: no cherry or sandalwood or mahogany here; just as in the next image the pair is dehumanized by an implied conjunction with the dice through an echo of the common expression "ein Paar Würfel," and also by having its presumably amorous activities designated with a crisp biological word, "Ansaugestadium." This word, however, the first of the poem's series of abstract terms, by its length, by its comparative metrical richness, and by its rhythmic position at the end of one of two "blank verse" lines, prepares for the ironic and rhythmically expansive bravura of the third line ("mit einem Kastanienast auf dem Klavier tritt die Natur hinzu.").

"Die Natur" for the "Paar" is doubtless *wunderschön,* and so is the music of the "Klavier."* For Benn, "die Natur" has the inexorability of the processes which in the next two stanzas dizzy humanity —and himself (there are no identifying pronouns for us to choose which). "Die Natur"; the accent falls heavily on this word, as it does on the other nouns ("Nebenzimmer," "Würfel," "Holztisch," "Paar," "Ansaugestadium," "Kastanienast," and "Klavier"; not to mention "Milieu"). *Natur*—a word whose meanings scholars have busied themselves like ants to heap into a historical maze—splendid

---

*We are reminded of the yearning throngs in the German newspapers' marriage advertisements, who tell us they love *Musik* and *Natur.*

exemplum of Benn's orthodox modernist view of words: "Worte schlagen mehr an als die Nachricht und den Inhalt, sie sind einerseits Geist, aber haben andererseits das Wesenhafte und Zweideutige der Dinge der Natur."[5] (Words sound to more than reportage or content; on the one hand they are intellect [*Geist*], but on the other hand they have the existent quality and the ambiguity of things in nature.)

We must not, in this instance, busy ourselves after mere "Nachricht" or "Inhalt." They are there, but in the background. Whether the couple throw the dice, whether they play the "Klavier" or listen to it, whether they set the stage with the branch, whether Benn can actually see them—these are questions not so much distracting as falsifying. The words are not symbols but ambiguous existences, like the "Milieu," at whose disjunctions what goes on in the next stanza comes about:

> Da versinken die Denkprozesse,
> die Seekrankheit, die einem tagsüber
> die Brechzentren bearbeitet,
> gehn unter in Alkohol und Nebulosem—
> endlich Daseinschwund und Seelenausglanz!

The poem is a "Seekrankheit." It is itself a congeries of "Brechzentren" (centers of explosion or vomiting), a "Notturno," which Benn on principle would not want to make a less disturbing, less disordered "Denkprozess," any more than would the composer of "Notturnos," Chopin, in the poem Benn has written about him:

> wenn Delacroix Theorien entwickelte
> wurde er unruhig, er seinerseits konnte
> die Notturnos nicht begründen.[6]

> If Delacroix developed theories,
> he became restless, he for his part could
> not base the Nocturnes.

We may attribute to Benn here too the words with which he concludes the poem on Chopin:

> Nie eine Oper Komponiert,
> keine Symphonie,
> nur diese tragischen Progressionen
> aus artistischer Überzeugung
> und mit einer kleinen Hand.

> Never composed an opera,
> No symphony,
> only these tragic progressions
> from artistic conviction
> and with a small hand.

"Diese tragische Progressionen," here, in Benn's own "Notturno," move from love through seasickness to the primal oceans before consciousness and conception. First, three concrete urban images, then a condition of body and spirit ("Seekrankheit, endlich Daseinschwund und Seelenausglanz"), then a kind of questioning resignation. There is a diffusion of statement, a play of tone, among the three parts of the poem, as in the three images from which it sets out. A tentative poem, deliberately so, an improvisation of artistic words, a "Notturno." The poem is coming to terms with an immense question, a "Zeitfrage," by at once dismissing it and giving in to it in a physical response that may—or may not—really prefigure the end of time. "Keiner fischte ihre Ungeheuer,/keiner litt tiefer als drei Meter/ und das ist wenig." The poet comes to terms with an outrageous infinity, an "Ungeheuer," with his tiny three meters of the sea of existence, by suggesting a greater diffusion through a smaller. "Das ist wenig" puts into abstract language what the disjunction of the initial three images implied. Here the "Brechzentren" of the pleasure principle are questions about the death principle. As Benn had said near the end of "Zur Problematik des Dichterischen," "If others would like to speak, between the lines and without a gap, of things which came into existence only later, to depict relationships

which pass away, to live for questions which quickly fall to pieces—
ever and at all times will that return for which all life is only a call
out of the deep, an old and early deep, and everything transitory
only a likeness of an unknown primal experience that seeks remem-
brances in it for itself." Then, a "dark, an inviolable Whole." And
finally, "your song is threatening as the star vault, beginning and
end perpetually the same." Or as Benn put it in one of his shorter
poems, "All is shore. Eternal calls the sea," "Alles ist Ufer. Ewig
ruft das Meer."[7]

A "Notturno" is music. Diffuse images attract diffuse meters, and
vice versa. Here, just as the words have a hard, dry assuredness that
aches for the symbols and order they are really evading, so one cannot find in these rhythms any abstract pattern, syllabic or accentual,
to which the poem even half conforms. There is no superimposed
order of sound, just as there is none of sense. Each is a "tragische
Progression." The first two lines do set an iambic pentameter norm
definitely enough, and it is sufficiently returned to at least once in
each stanza, so that the rest of the poem sounds like disappointed
blank verse. But that is part of the trick. Actually we have only to
mark the major accents in a line, or to mark accents at all, even in
these lines of near blank verse, to realize that strange attractions are
tugging at the sounds of the poem.

> Im Nébenzímmer die Würfel auf den Hólztísch,
> benáchbart ein Paár ím Ansáugestádium . . .
> éndlích Dáseinschwúnd und Seélenaúsglanz.

(Here I mean the acute accents over italicized vowels to represent
heavy stress, and those over roman vowels to represent light stress.)
The rhythms are not approximations of a pattern; they are variable
fields of force. We end with the short dissonance of "und das ist
wenig," where (every one of the first four?) syllables may be seen as
more or less heavily accented depending on one's definition of the
field which the poem's achievement is to succeed in leaving undefined. The openness of the rhythms lets them through, so to speak,

to the meaning of the poem. Another of Benn's remarks may shed light on this point. "Wenn Sie vom Gereimten das Stimmungsmässige abziehen, was dann übrigbleibt, wenn dann noch etwas übrigbleibt, das ist dann vielleicht ein Gedicht."[8] (If you take the tonal mean away from verses, what is left over—if anything is left over—will then perhaps be a poem.)

William Carlos Williams relies on a diffuse organization so seemingly close to the current of everyday perceptions as to be nearly neutral in tone, occasioning neither Benn's abrupt transitions nor Whitman's excitement. In his poem "The Poor," the rhythms, though lighter and somewhat more regular than those of "Notturno," follow the contours of speech, the abstracted near chaos of the actual voice, and avoid the canons of rhythm toward a similar end:

> It's the anarchy of poverty
> delights me, the old
> yellow wooden house indented
> among the new brick tenements
>
> Or a cast iron balcony
> with panels showing oak branches
> in full leaf. It fits
> the dress of the children
>
> reflecting every stage and
> custom of necessity—
> Chimneys, roofs, fences of
> wood and metal in an unfenced
>
> age and enclosing next to
> nothing at all: the old man
> in a sweater and soft black
> hat who sweeps the sidewalk—
>
> his own ten feet of it—
> in a wind that fitfully
> turning his corner has
> overwhelmed the entire city.[9]

Through the years Williams has argued against using the classical rhythms of English, and the emphasis of that American voice appears throughout in the stresses of this poem. "It's the ánarchy of poverty," and so on. The poem might almost be said to build itself loosely within these four-line stanzas in order to set up a portable concert room for each cadence of meandering voice. Similarly, if I may anticipate, the rhythms of Montale's poem are freer of meter, in order to follow the bluster and self-infusion of the waters he writes about. And the lines of Reverdy drift without punctuation through the dissolving half-metaphors of his half-apocalypse.

Williams in his poem is approaching personally and genially a human condition, poverty, which is fundamental and hard-pressed, fundamental because hard-pressed. But Williams is not interested or delighted in the sentiments which the word's overtones may carry (that is, these overtones are there but he does not develop them). He attends to the effects of poverty on what the eye can see, human beings leaving their anarchic mark on a nature which other poems of Williams express as being equally anarchic. "When a man makes a poem," Williams says, "makes it, mind you, he takes words as he finds them interrelated about him and composes them—without distortion which would mar their exact significances—into an intense expression of their perceptions and ardors."

In each of these stanzas we are presented with one or more human beings and also with one or more man-made objects in a landscape. In the first stanza the human being is Williams, the objects an old yellow house "indented"—like the beginning of a paragraph—among new, *the* new brick tenements. The article gives extra finality to the "new" but is less demonstrative than "those" would be; Williams wishes the words to make the tenement sound inevitable without giving this image special prominence. In the second stanza the object comes first, an instance of anarchy. "Die Natur" can "hinzutreten" only in the form of a cast iron oak branch on a balcony. The branch is in full leaf, at a perpetual height, like the children whose dress therefore "it fits" (the antecedent of "it" is ambiguous, being also anarchy, not to say also the general situation of the poem). In this stanza the human beings are these children, and their dress is continued into the third stanza with the poem's full set of abstractions, clothing their innocence, as it were, by giving compass bearings on their anarchy:

> It fits
> the dress of the children
>
> reflecting every stage and
> custom of necessity—
> Chimney, roofs, fences of
> wood and metal.

"It fits" for the reason that scene, anarchy, and dress, all reflect every stage and custom of necessity. Note that Williams as he says "the" tenements uses the participle, "reflecting," and not "because it reflects" or "in order to reflect," or any other schema for the abstractions which then stand in their inviolable paratactic equality as an anatomy of anarchy: stage and custom of necessity. Custom may include stage, stage may include custom, by necessity so to speak, but again we have a simple copula, "stage and custom." The genitive "of necessity" goes equally with both; and it is both objective and subjective genitive at once, or rather is so primal in its presentation as to be strictly neither.

Only a dash can cover the distance to the next perception—a dash of the sort dear to modern poets from Emily Dickinson on. The dash bridges the gap from abstractions to diffuse objects. For the humanity of children in this third stanza, our objects are the protective parts of houses, those that let out smoke and keep off rain and keep out intruders, "chimneys, roofs, fences." But the anarchic weather is too penetrating to be kept off; behind the fences in the fourth stanza which enclose next to nothing at all, we have an old man, a single person, while the children were plural, whose dress is concrete while theirs was abstract, "a sweater and soft black hat." The man is "old," as was the yellow wooden house. (Williams somewhere remarks that one must always have justification for repeating a word in a poem.) Here, as in the poetry of Rilke, normally mature human beings, except for the poet's persona, are absent. We have only those so innocent or so old and beyond caring as to be completely attuned to anarchy. The black of the old man's hat is a still more abstract color than the yellow of the wooden house; and he is absorbed in the rather abstract act of doing homage to anarchy by a ritual of order, sweeping his own ten feet of sidewalk, as tiny a space as Benn's "drei Meter." He sweeps on into the fifth, final stanza, where the visible object balancing his humanity is not tenements or balcony or fence, but no less than the entire city the wind has overwhelmed. He has stature enough in his very subservience to the petty needs of life to master anarchy, as the poem is doing.

For consider: on which side of the fence is the old man sweeping? Syntax has him inside the fence, "enclosing next to nothing at all: the old man." But sense tells us that he is outside the fence, where sidewalks usually are; it is probably not the private sidewalk that leads to the door, or Williams would not have said "his own ten feet of it." He cannot be both inside and outside, but in an "unfenced age" it depends on your point of view. He is enclosed out outside, which makes sense only when you perceive that spatial anarchy is a kind of order. "Say it/ no ideas but in things" Williams asserts, meaning thereby not that there are no ideas, but that ideas are in things, here one idea in a group of diffuse things. Williams through these diffuse images has created an idea, an apperception which is painterly—a city quarter of indefinite length with yellow, black, cast iron, and brick, variegations of dress—; and at the same time this apperception is intellectual, defining anarchy, custom, necessity, stage, as interwoven with the eye and the heart.

More closely allied to Romantic traditions is Eugenio Montale. The poem of his that I cite so pulses with its occasion that it is given no name; it stresses the furtive union between his personal self and nature by presenting the diffuse images of a few moments by the sea.

The poem comes from a book section entitled "Mediterraneo," the name of a sea whose root implication places it at the land's center; here, as in Benn, it is perhaps also a "Brechzentrum." And the title of the book is *Ossi di Seppia*, cuttlefish bones. The cuttlefish is of such softness in his drift through the sea that we think of him as having no bones: like him these drifting poems, ejecting as do cuttlefish their brown ink over a small diffuse area of a sea of images, do without a rational spine.*

This poem begins with a *vortice*, a whirl:

> A vortice s'abbatte
> sul mio capo reclinato
> un suono d'agri lazzi.
> Scotta la terra percorsa
> da sghembe ombre di pinastri,
> e al mare là in fondo fa velo
> piú che i rami, allo sguardo, l'afa che a tratti
>   erompe
> dal suolo che si avvena.
> Quando piú sordo o meno il ribollio dell' acque
> che s'ingorgano
> accanto a lunghe secche mi raggiunge:
> o è un bombo talvolta ed un ripiovere
> di schiume sulle rocce.
> Come rialzo il viso, ecco cessare
> i ragli** sul mio capo; e scoccare
> verso le strepeanti acque,
> frecciate biancazzure, due ghiandaie.[10]

> In a whirl there plunges
> upon my reclined head
> a sound of sharp buffooneries.
> The earth stings, traversed

*My dictionary, though, specifies that cuttlefish differ from squid "in having a calcified internal shell, cuttle bone, used for polishing, powder, bird food, etc." So these poems are presumably to be thought of as internal shells useful for ornament, and for nourishment.

**The Mondadori edition reads thus. Perhaps *ragli* is a misprint for *raggi*, rays.

by skew shadows of big fir trees,
and on the sea, there below, it makes a veil
more than the branches, to the glance, the
            sultriness that in starts erupts
from the ground that suits it.
When deafer or less, the surf of the waters
that choke up
beside dry lengths rejoins me:
or there is a roaring sometimes and a raining
of scum over the rocks.
As I lift my gaze: see cease
the brays over my head; and fly out
toward the blustering waters,
blue-white arrow shots, two jaybirds.

The poet's self is presented in relation to happenings with objects in nature that are as diffuse, as askew, "sghembe," as the shadows of the big fir trees. Here again, as in Williams and Benn, to call these objects metaphors or symbols would falsify their literal immediacy. The poet carefully refrains from metaphor until the playful explosion, the "lazzo," "buffoonery" of the last line: "frecciate biancazzure," silver-white arrow shots, the metaphor; and then immediately what it designates, "due ghiandaie," two jaybirds. They are arrow shots because they visually appear so as they fly out or seem to fly out toward the sea. This has happened because the poet has shifted his reclined head: one motion has ceased, the brays, "ragli," upon his head; and something else has flown out, "due ghiandaie"; because he lifted his gaze. The relation between self and nature in the poem is immediate, and at the same time radically puzzling. The "due ghiandaie" leave us in the air, final and trivial both together. What we have again is a small "tragische Progression" won from an infinity. Here, even more than in our other poems, the self is defined by what it is not: the poet's feeling is buried in the landscape that rejoins him, "mi raggiunge," in the form of surf, a momentary whiteness of waters. "Je est un autre" (I is another), Rimbaud said, or, to

quote the words of the poem with which Montale began the original
collection *Ossi di Seppia:*

> Non chiederci la parola che squadri da ogni lato
> l'animo nostro informe, e a lettere di fuoco
> lo dichiari e risplenda come un croco
> perduto in mezzo a un polveroso prato.
>
> . . . .
>
> Non domandarci la formula che mondi possa aprirti
> sí qualche storta sillaba e secha come un ramo.
> Codesto solo oggi possiamo dirti,
> ciò che *non* siamo, ciò che *non* vogliamo.[11]

> Do not ask us for the word that would square from every side
> Our unformed soul, and in letters of fire
> clarify it and shine like a crocus
> lost in the middle of a dusty meadow.
>
> . . . .
>
> Demand not of us the formula that could open worlds for you,
> such a distorted syllable, dry as a branch.
> This only can we tell you today,
> That which we are *not*, that which we do *not* want.

A person knows himself here by diffuse hints from what he is not,
the outer world.

In the following poem of Reverdy, too, we are given only glimmers,
"Lueurs." Like Benn, Williams, and Montale, Reverdy makes his
rhythms up as he goes along. Here he gets a feeling well-nigh dream-
like into the rhythms by omitting all punctuation. Even more than
in Mallarmé and Apollinaire, from whom he borrows this practice,
we cannot establish in Reverdy the points of sentences. Lines are
sentences and at the same time appositional clauses rephrasing each
other. Each of the diffuse images comes to the same thing, or is a
different flicker, a "lueur," of the same meaning. Reverdy has put
his poem together as a "machine of words" (the original phrase is
Valéry's, adopted by Williams and paralleled by Benn); he calls his

life work by the title of *Main d'Oeuvre,* handiwork. So composed is
the poem's contemplation of self and nature that it is abstract to
the point of mystery:

LUEURS

On sait que les feux se rejoindront
dans l'ombre et au même moment
qu'il faudra répéter la formule de vie
devant le ciel ridé et presque éteint
Les étoiles perdues brûlent en descendant
La lune est noyée dans l'étang
Tous les êtres repris se reculent ensemble
Les voix qui chantent se ressemblent
Tous les esprits montent très haut
par une seule voie
Les arbres secoués par un courant d'en bas
A mi-chemin ont lieu les mauvaises rencontres
Les maisons arrachées sans mal
comme des dents
Il reste quelques trous dans la terre
Et rien dedans
Une minute
Où règne l'immobilité absolue
Le silence avant l'effondrement
Sur le chemin découvert et à peine aperçu
Le berger s'en allait ayant perdu ses bêtes
On croyait qu'il pleurait en remuant la tête
Devant son troupeau de nuages
Et tout ce qui restait du monde
Après l'orage[12]

GLIMMERS

It is known that the fires will come together
in the shadow and at the same moment
that it will be necessary to repeat the formula of life
before the wrinkled and almost extinguished sky
The lost stars burn going down
The moon is drowned in a pool
All the retaken beings draw back together

The voices that sing resemble each other
All the spirits climb very high
by a single way
The trees shaken by a current from below
In mid-passage take place the bad encounters
The houses pulled up without pain
like teeth
There remain some holes in the earth
And nothing inside
A minute
When absolute immobility reigns
The silence before the downfall
On the road uncovered and scarcely perceived
The shepherd was going away having lost his beasts
He was thought to be crying while moving his head
Before his flock of clouds
And all that remained of the world
After the storm

Quasi-abstract, quasi-metaphoric, the words of this poem have an even more generalized quality than is usual in French poetic diction. In one sense everything is literal, a series of statements mostly elliptical about the way things look after a storm, "après l'orage," the last line of the poem revealing the thread. The fires coming together suggest the look of twilight after a storm. So do the lost stars, the moon drowned in the pond, the trees in the wind. The encounters would be bad in the middle of the road because it is wet from the storm. Since the flock of the last long image turns out to be clouds, their shepherd in this light would be the sun, his tears rain.

Taken this way the abstract metaphors are a veiled reference to something quite concrete: the shepherd is a sun. Taken another way, the metaphors are more abstract, vaguely portentous, apocalyptic. Then the fires are themselves "lueurs," offglancings of an apocalyptic light. The storm is a spiritual condition. The shepherd would be Man herding nature, or God, or the poet, or just a wandering image diffusely separated from other images, going away for the same reason that the stars are lost and the moon is drowned. All the retaken beings draw together, though all the spirits climb high, and by a single way, the way of the poem. Williams' city was overwhelmed by winds, and Reverdy, in a volume whose title is *Sources des Vents*, sources of the winds, traces the anarchy of winds, a storm, to an intimation of cosmic events. For all of these poets have expressed through their diffuse images something like an apocalypse. All are of a time which Yeats summarized in perhaps the best known of poetic apocalypses. "The Second Coming": "Things fall apart. The center cannot hold./Mere anarchy is loosed upon the world."

When things fall apart, the poet may stare at the disjoined things themselves. In these terms Perse characterizes modern poetry: "It feels it is not really poetry unless it merges with its living object in a live embrace, unless it informs the object entirely and even becomes part of its very substance. . . . This poetry lives the thing and 'animates' it totally and must scrupulously and with infinite variation submit to the thing's own measure and rhythm."[13] Perse has in mind particular objects; but in his own diffuse practice, as in that of the poets we have been discussing, a particular object comes to the consciousness only through the poet's struggle with the double task of fixing it in a stasis while understanding it in the larger flux. Self and Nature interpenetrate, so immediately that Aristotle's notion of imitation could not begin to cover the relations. Though Poe and others have made quasi-theological statements about the poetic act, it would be a mistake to read diffusion as the fidelity to nature of an Ersatz Scripture. The self-persona of Yeats or Pound, the *Ich* of Benn, the *Je* of Rimbaud, is too much a construct, and too involved in flux, to appear primarily in the ultimately defining religious light. Baudelaire uses "temple" in a classical, and metaphorical (not Christian) sense, in his lines on this subject: "La Nature est un temple où de vivants piliers/ Laissent parfais sortir de confuses paroles."[14]

In using diffusion, the poet attempts an immediate, intuitive grasp of the relation between self and nature by refusing to provide a logical structure for either. Whereas earlier poetry created a musical order through canons of meter and idea, modern poetry makes up its rhythms as it goes along: its units of idea are the atoms of words, and the diffusion of images signalizes the precariousness, the momentary character, of the order made by the poem.

For the flux of the self, as of nature, Baudelaire also provides key terms. He says in *Mon Coeur Mis à Nu*, "De la vaporisation et de la centralization du *Moi*. Tout est là." The vaporization and the centralization of the Ego. Everything is there.

Vaporization and centralization constitute poles of the same "*Moi*." So poets who vaporize with diffusion of images, and poets who centralize through strict control over a single image, are approaching the same problem from two different directions. It is because of their centralization in the midst of a consciously resisted flux that the modern poem of severe control and exclusive statement seems far more airtight than its romantic or classic prototypes. Baudelaire, Mallarmé, George, Valéry, Rilke, hermetically triumph over flux by setting up its opposite, the stasis of a perilously poised poem. And even their poems strain toward the flux of diffusion. Valéry's "Cimetière Marin," a meditation like Montale's poem about the self by the sea, concentrates on a single cemetery at a single moment; still, it ranges from "rooftops" to "doves" to open water; and it contemplates with anguish the paradox of stasis and flux in the parables of Zeno of Elea: "Zénon, cruel Zénon, Zénon d' Elée." Rilke will break out of his poem's tight frame at the end of "Archaischer Torso Apollos" to address the Self suddenly: "Du musst dein Leben ändern," You must change your life.

One can triumph over flux and defeat mere stasis in a poem either by mastering flux through keeping time with it in diffuse images or by banishing flux as utterly as possible from the total artifice of the work. Modernism in poetry is not so much a tradition of diffusion or concentration as it is a condition of living, of knowing, in which the poet, sometimes heroically but always strenuously, tries to come to terms with living and knowing in a fusion so faithful to both that it will not admit the finality of either classical rhetoric or romantic tonal (and mythic) unity.*

A third way, so arduous that only poetry of the rarest illustriousness could attempt it, is to remain orphically open toward both flux and stasis. The flux of diffusion, the stasis of concentration—they seem exclusive. But it is possible to set up a rigid form,—the sonnet, say,—to return again and again to one theme; and yet to flow diffusely through integers of poetic experience: Rilke's *Sonnets to Orpheus*. It is toward this fusing way that Rilke exhorts us—and himself—in the last lines of that marvelous sequence, which does manage the advantages of both diffusion and concentration:

> Sei in dieser Nacht aus Übermass
> Zauberkraft am Kreuzweg deiner Sinne,
> ihrer seltsamen Begegnung Sinn.
>
> Und wenn dich das Irdische vergass,
> zu der stillen Erde sag: Ich rinne.
> Zu dem raschen Wasser sprich: ich bin.[15]
>
> Be in this night from excess
> Magic at the crossroad of your sense,
> Of your own strange meeting sense.
>
> And if the earthly forget you,
> To the still earth say: I run.
> To the swift water speak: I am.

*At the moment in America many are responsive to this demand: Koch, Ashbery, Ginsberg, Creeley, Olson, Levertov, Logan, Touster, Stanley Moss, Feldman, to name just a few, joined afresh by poets like Simpson and Merwin as these have broken the chrysalis of a more conventional style.

GENERALITY:
THE OPEN BOOK

In "LUEURS" Reverdy keeps the sense of his poem open by organizing it in a diffuse way. Thereby he is impelled towards a generality different from the kind sought by the classical writer, whose plot we can generalize by extrapolation (Oedipus is all men), or whose statements carry a gnomic force ("The Flower in the Crannied Wall" purports to include all experience in its reference). Reverdy's poem is indeterminate; we therefore cannot extrapolate from it or put it to more than provisional gnomic uses. In his work, as in that of many modern writers, the very class words in the dictionary, while under pressure for carrying a generality of cognitive and emotional burden, are pressed into a service that does not classify in an ordinary sense. Normal designations are bypassed (*l'orage* is, and is not, a rainstorm) not to avoid the generality implied by class words—by "universals" in the old sense—but to achieve another, more open, kind of generality.

Pope's diction, or even Shakespeare's, consists, notably and for a large part, of class words, exploited so as to exhibit a generality that is both explicit and classifiable. In the *Essay on Man* Pope announces his generality as he announces his subject:

> Know then thyself, presume not God to scan;
> The proper study of Mankind is Man.

The end-stopped couplet all by itself conveys an impression of completeness-in-limitation. Closing off as it does with a rhyme, this particular aphorism carries none of the openness that is suggested in the gnomic sentences of Heraclitus, or René Char. Again, the very mystery that resides in mankind is summed up by Pope in a triad of allegations, and the syntactic equivalence of these three nouns insists on the completeness, and so delimitation, of the summary:

The glory, jest, and riddle of the world!

Whether we exalt man, laugh at him, or puzzle over him, we know him, Pope implies, in the act of designating him "glory," "jest," or "riddle." Pope, of course, says not "or," but "and," presenting thereby not three enigmatic alternatives but an exhaustive series of three general names.

Even when it rises to Shakespeare's richness of allusion, the language of "classical" poetry implies classification, and derives from or even embodies some sort of stable relation between the parts of the world designated by its words and the conception of a coherent whole. In our time the instability of the whole may be seen not only in the diffusion of one poem, or the concentration of another; it appears in the very generality of the best literary language, a generality beyond either Empson's kinds of ambiguity or the perhaps necessarily polysemous character of literary works generally. Dante, who applies the word "polysemous" to his work, has four levels; in modern work, often, it is as though the poet pulled away from levels and multiplicities to present a mysterious unity, a generality that allows no stable part-whole relation, however complex. We are not able definitely to construct, for such modern works, in the terminology of P. E. Strawson,[16] subject-predicate relations between particulars and universals that attribute, or that characterize, or that classify by sorting.

To put it another way, the recent poet's language relates first to his own internal fluctuations, a concern that begins to figure prominently in the program of the Romantic poet. Knowing the world, for Wordsworth, entailed knowing himself. Yet far from taking Pope's Socratic injunction—"Know then thyself"—for granted, he postponed a larger statement about the world till after he had gone over himself in *The Prelude*. He resigned himself, finally, to letting the main music remain unheard, by going over just *The Prelude* again almost half a century later.

Man is the poet: *The Prelude* presents "the growth of a poet's mind." The poem sees the generality of human existence as especially characterized by its speaking of that generality, of "praising" it inclusively "to the end." For Rilke, similarly, any song finally rises from, and is, "Orpheus":

> Ein für alle Male
> ists Orpheus wenn es singt[17]

As Orpheus, the poet-knowing-man, dies into humanity, mankind becomes one with the world by being a "mouth of nature,"

> Nur weil dich reissend zuletzt die Feindschaft verteilte,
> sind wir die Hörenden jetzt und ein Mund der Natur.[18]

> Now since at last hate tears you and parcels you out,
> Are we the listeners now and a mouth of nature.

While theorists, like the Poe of *Eureka*, proclaim a new burden of philosophical generality for the poem, the world which the poem envisages and even includes may be seen to surpass the poem, keeping by definition a step ahead of the poem. The worship of Baudelaire's poet at the temple of nature evokes sybilline utterances only sometimes ("parfois"), and even then the words are "confusing":

> La nature est un temple où de vivant piliers
> Laissent parfois sortir de confuses paroles.

For Whitman, beginning with the self entails breaking the particulars of nature down into "leaves of grass." In the "Song of Myself," the act of ritual praise, "celebration," when it is one with the act of song, amounts to a loose foundation of future presupposition, "what I assume you shall assume." This, in turn, necessarily ("for") involves the smallest integral units of a person's being:

> I celebrate myself, and sing myself,
> And what I assume you shall assume,
> For every atom belonging to me as good belongs to you.[19]

The fullness of the world, which the long incantatory lines seem to be striving to sum up name by name, lulls the poet and keeps forever, by the poem's own definition, a step ahead of him. He speaks from that fullness, while it encompasses him; he is like an infant who resists being put to sleep, "out of the cradle endlessly rocking."

The generality which the poet seeks, exceeds the poet's grasp. And the excess gets built into the poem as another way of hinting at the generality. Keeping the book open. Reverdy's "Lueurs" evades being a poem about the weather, or the sun going behind clouds, or an internal vision. Nor would it be right to say that the poem includes these and several other possible plots, either alternately, or simultaneously. Such an assertion of multiple interpretation, or of ambiguity, in being applicable to any work of literature at all, would fail to point up Reverdy's own special "evasion" of any particular designations, of normal sets of relations among his given terms. His poem strains to get beyond even the summary statement that the weather of the world is that of the soul. In aspiring to keep the book of the poem open, it foregoes the generalities of ordinary syntax, it surrenders the designations of ordinary language (which initially either points, or does not point, at a real *designatum*, cloud or sun).

The language of narrative fiction itself, while tied by story-sequence more tightly to its *designata*, has been made in our time to bear a generality of theme that Trollope and Dickens would have found puzzling. Hemingway's "simple" style, for example, gains its intensity from the condensations of feeling he is trying to generalize, and to keep general. He leaves unstated, and so assumes, a general feeling on which the particulars draw at the same time that their effects, by a kind of preterition, are suggesting it. Simplifying the language highlights the act of leaving the general feeling unstated:

> It was late and everyone had left the cafe except an old man who sat in the shadow the leaves of the tree made against the electric light. In the daytime the street was dusty, but at night the dew settled the dust and the old man liked to sit late be-

cause he was deaf and now at night it was quiet and he felt the
difference. The two waiters inside the cafe knew that the old
man was a little drunk, and while he was a good client they
knew that if he became too drunk he would leave without
paying, so they kept watch on him.[20]

Here the simple declarative sentences set onto one level a physical
effect ("the dew settled the dust") and an emotional response ("the
old man liked to sit late"), unifying them. No comma is provided
before the "and" that joins these two statements to mitigate their
syntactic likeness, and a scantness of punctuation throughout sub-
serves the deliberate paratactic monotony. As a method, this style
elsewhere advertises the restrictedness of its diction, its shrinking to
a single, and general monochrome the whole spectrum of abstractions for which such words as "liked" and "felt" do simple and
summary duty. "Felt the difference" generalizes the scene, because
the old man, being deaf, must deduce the quiet of the scene from its
other attributes: the emptiness of the cafe, the dew on the settled
dust, the electric light on the leaves. The leap from a night emptiness that is seen to a night quiet that is not heard becomes the first
term for the leap between a visible scene that is scrupulously item-
ized and an all-embracing mood ("despair") that is deliberately left
unstated—except backhandedly at the end when the waiter substitutes a cryptic (Spanish) word, "nothing," for many key words in
The Lord's Prayer. One could, as a kind of historical exercise, con-
vert this story's despair into *Angst*, the nothing into *Nicht-sein* or
néant. And one could call the old waiter's "probable insomnia" the
wakefulness of a man who senses mortality (an old man in the void
between the *Sein* of his existence and the *Seiende* of a world the
other old man's deafness shuts him off—and does not shut him off—
from apprehending). However, to import the existentialist nomen-
clature would be merely to provide another verbal structure for what
ought to be apprehended by attention to the verbal structure at
hand. The story will not name its feeling except negatively, "not fear
or dread . . . a nothing that he knew too well," as it will not specify

the people—to say nothing of the city or the cafe—by giving them any names. The old man is anonymous anyway to the old waiter, which no more prevents the old waiter from intuitively understanding him than deafness prevents the old man from deducing, and liking, quiet.

The last sentence of the story has the waiter apply "insomnia" generally to an undetermined multitude ("Many") in a colloquial word ("must") that blends easy conjecture with an idea of necessity, "many must have it."

One cannot call this story's tone ironic, or not ironic, so little does it partake of the classifying assumptions on which any ironic schema must initially be built. In all the range of tonal possibilities for irony that our literature provides, one can always find at their base the simple formula of verbal irony, a statement made through its contradiction, whereby a complaint about nasty weather is phrased as "It's a fine day!" To say "this is a clean room," is ironic when one means the room is dirty. But in order to say it, one must have a coherent notion of what constitutes dirtiness. That the cafe is actually a clean well-lighted place, and is called such, keeps from the designation of the title the irony which at the same time is sensed in the disproportion between an unstated whole life and the stated satisfaction of a place fleetingly visited. We feel the title to be ironic, even though we cannot test its particular attributions against an implied (counter-) assertive base.

Through such simple and radical means does this story generalize its theme. It is about nothing less than the human condition—and not even "the modern condition," because, though we may say this, *it* does not. While Henry James focuses on a moral problem and Jane Austen on a moral education, Hemingway does not focus, but hovers, as his irony may be said to hover, in a generality which his style postulates as more inclusive than even a vast novel in an older convention may be, *La Comédie Humaine*, *War and Peace*. This is a human comedy, but a tragedy, too, without the alternation between comedy and tragedy that moral and societal foci involve.

Here, instead of morality, we are given a general feeling; and instead of society, an isolated man, utterly unique and utterly typical.

Literature, Merleau-Ponty says, contains matrices of ideas rather than ideas themselves. ("l'oeuvre d'art . . . contient, mieux que des idées, des matrices d'idées, [et] elle nous fournit d'emblèmes . . .")[21] Hemingway is faithful to this attribution, as faithful in his brief stories as Joyce is in the expanse of *Finnegans Wake*.

In poetic language, once again, we can see such generality more flamboyantly at work. In Montale's brief poem about a rising wind, "Lungomare," the diffusion of particulars in an arbitrary event has the effect of intensifying the feeling of the poem, and suspending its metaphors, into a generality that a classic form, the hendecasyllabic tercet, does not close but leaves hanging:

> Il soffio cresce, il buio è rotto a squarci,
> e l'ombra che tu mandi sulla fragile
> palizzata s'arriccia. Troppo tardi
>
> se vuoi esser te stessa! Della palma
> tonfa il sorcio, il baleno è sulla miccia,
> sui lunghissimi cigli del tuo squardo.[22]

SEASIDE PROMENADE

> The gust grows, the dark is broken in fragments,
> and the shadow that you throw on the fragile
> palissade frizzles up. Too late
>
> if you wish to be yourself! From the palm
> plops the mouse, the lightning is on the wick,
> on the longest lashes of your look.

As often in poetry, many of these words contain the sort of denotational and connotational complexity that Empson (*The Structure of Complex Words*) unravels for "honest" in *Othello* or "sense" in *The Prelude* "—mare," "cresce," "buio," "rotto," "ombra," to go no farther, comprise, each of them, whole resonances of philosophic and emotional force. That connotative force is kept, by the diffusion of the statements, from functioning as mere descriptive designation of wind by the sea. Words are signs, but in poems of this sort the ordinary designations point only incidentally at objects and events. "—mare," but we hear no more about the sea; and the romantic intensity of that word is left open, not being closed by the syntax. "*Lungomare*": a place, where what happens is cosmic as lightning and trivial as a wick, and the "self" is always "too late" "to be."

The syntactic disjunctions from phrase to phrase keep the complex connotations of the individual words from engendering any closed, explicable event or sign-system of the sort furnished (however complexly) by, say, *Othello* or *The Prelude*. Up to a simple and momentary happening, a gust of wind at night, float the packed words, one by one. Each word, in its disjunct solitude, can unload from its whole pack of connotation only the base denotation required for mere narrative. In the disparity between the force these resonant words might have and the broken designations the diffusion allows them, resides the feeling of the poem, as general through the "undischarged" force of the complex words as the event is particular in its simple, physical occurrence. Here words are "glass," as Montale has called them. While the intensity of the poem suggests a metaphoric charge, there are no schematic metaphors in any ordinary sense, because vehicle and tenor, like the vehicle-tenor relationship itself, cannot become schematized: the poem gives them nothing to be hung on. The one movement of repeated variation crosses from the subdued compound preposition in the title, "Lungo-," to the expanded superlative that dominates the last line, "lunghissimi." Semi-metaphoric words, "mandi," "s'arriccia," dissolve into mere colloquial turns of phrase, so that the social structure of "command" or the metaphoric vehicle of "curling" hair cannot be included definitely in the picture. Or excluded.

Hence we cannot begin analysis by saying that some general point is the tenor of a schematized metaphor and the gust of wind a particular vehicle thereof. Or vice versa. Its fixation on a particular, even trivial instance, the gust of wind by night, renders the generality of the poem ineluctable because it cannot be brought into proportionate representation. Experience, something small, and a feeling, something large, find a connection in the fact that at no point is there a scale, of smallness or of largeness, in which a small experience and a large feeling can meet, by which they can be defined. The generality of the poem's feeling remains open just because the event of the poem is so delimited.

The single instance focused on in such poems is not subsumed under a general observation. The air of generality is raised through the presentation of something singular. Similarly the beasts in Marianne Moore's poems, elephants or snails, cannot serve simply, schematically, as metaphors of the human condition because the attention remains focussed so painstakingly on *their* perceptible attributes. They are nothing if not seen. The elusive austerity of her poems, the abstract diction, the insistence on pointing a moral, the exact calibrations of a metre counted out syllable by syllable, all contrive an occasion which pretends to be complete in itself (the abstractness of the diction aids the illusion of inclusiveness) and at the same time specific. Completeness and specificity are found, though, in miniature; or in the announced fragmentariness of "Part of a Novel, Part of a Poem, Part of a Play." (This title is dropped in her later collection as perhaps tipping the scale too much towards the disconnected particular.)

If the monkeys and the jerboa and the frigate pelican of her poems cannot be taken over wholly by their indeterminately suggested analogies to human kind, neither can they be called, in any strict sense, metonymic or synecdochic. There is no "other" fixity they can be related to, there is no whole they can be part of; and so the terms of classical rhetoric, metonymy or synecdoche, cannot be applied. The subject may be very particular; the theme is the more general. In the scholastic world of a medieval bestiary the moral is tagged onto the animal. In Marianne Moore's open world, the moral is given not as a conclusion but as a kind of counterbalance, or equivalent, of a fineness in the world of abstraction for the fineness of perception. As she says of "The Hero," ". . . He's not out/seeing a sight but the rock/crystal thing to see."[23] Her sea gets another name, not structurally a metaphor because it is an actual description, "A Grave"; there are really dead things under the sea.

That poem begins with a line of participial suspension:

> Man looking into the sea, . . .[24]

A series of visual *percepta,* rather trivial and disconnected, returns the poem to the sea while remaining perpetually short of the mortality that the title announces; and so the poem is about neither death nor visual observation (nor something connecting them both) but rather the general act of "consciousness" that might move through or into both; that is so doing in the poem; and that is negated in the last word of the poem. The end returns to the sea, but under a synonym "ocean":

> and the ocean, . . .
> advances as usual, looking as if it were not that ocean in which
>   dropped things are bound to sink—
> in which if they turn and twist, it is neither with volition
>   nor consciousness.[25]

The single instance, the "thing" spoken of in two of the passages just cited from her work, evokes generality by *not* being subsumed.

It is only in a poetic act of such generality that "things," the classically fixed or classifiable objects of sensory perception, can "take a stand," have a *parti pris.* Their stand is that the particularizing language can be conceived as moving around things infinitely, in a work like Francis Ponge's *Le Parti Pris des Choses,* a book of miniaturist descriptions which an existentialist philosopher can hail (Sartre, *Situations I*) as exhibiting the implications of a whole moral system. But Ponge's book ties in with programmatic existentialism most in its title. The poems themselves, again, rest austerely neutral. The hermetically concentrated specificity of their descriptions of orange or cigarette, rain or young mother, sunders them from any generality more committed than the faceless *"je"* who examines the objects. The first paragraph of "L'Orange" examines, without creating a simile, the attributes which an orange and a sponge have in common. The next paragraph moves back to ask the question of difference: "Faut-il prendre parti entre ces deux manières de mal supporter l'oppression?" And then the poem half answers the question in what amounts to another movement of consciousness. Between the dark progress of the verbalizing consciousness and the singleness of the thing it turns this way and that, rests not a *chosisme* or *Sachlichkeit*, but a poetic wholeness that insists on remaining free by pausing deliberately. This implied generality in the consciousness whose sequenced acts constitute the poem, precisely refuses to imitate things in the stance-taking specificity which it chronicles, as a kind of exorcism from making language do likewise. The words are then least like signs when most they seem to point. Description is a simple function of signs, but this description, in its deliberate simplicity, leaves its point hanging. Are the words themselves things, or signs of things? (Ponge himself, in his commentary *Méthodes*, makes much of the histories and flavors of words.) These poems are written on the other side of the specificity where that distinction functions meaningfully.

Ponge, to put it differently, bypasses metaphor (a kind of sign) by keeping the "thing" scrupulously in view. So his long poem "L'Araignée,"[26] without making the spider a figure for the intellect, can simultaneously miniaturize the world by peopling it with insects and schematize such human procedures as architecture and poetry, to name a pair in which Valéry found affinity. Yet the poem itself achieves a generality that does not permit its being read as an insect fable or a mind-metaphor: it offers neither Lilliput nor the spider in *The Battle of the Books*. The particular instance, a spider, does not signify this kind of classifying generality. The spider inheres in the generality; and the poem, with self-confident idiosyncracy and verve, celebrates that inherence.

Applying specific interpretations (Lilliput, mind-metaphor) and finding them insufficient, we are forced back to the specific "thing," and up to the generality. The generality will never be filled in by adding all the possible interpretations of the poem, because it includes them by implication rather than by addition. These are not parts that the whole poem in its sum exceeds. They are specific (and in a sense quite arbitrary) extensions of implications in the poem's structure. So there is no ambiguity of complementary interpretations: the language and syntax of "L'Araignée" provide no sets and classes to let us list, under the allegoric or metaphorical class "spider," the instance or aspect "Lilliput," or "mind-metaphor." Adherence to the particular "thing," the spider, broadens the generality of the poem's reference. An abstract word in the poem—and it is full of them—is held in balance between extravagant description of the insect and metaphoric indication of human intellection: a word becomes almost a thing in the extravagance of the first (a gratuitously big word looks like an embellished thing-in-itself), almost a sign in the cryptic designation of the second.

Ponge sustains the generality of a poem by pretending to do the opposite—to "describe" an object of scrupulously limited particularity. He carries this maneuver off neatly. But the tension between the general and the particular agonized Hopkins, and we can hear his internal *agon* in the "spring" of his rhythm. He went back all the way to Duns Scotus to get theological justification for reading God's oneness universally into the inscaped singularity, the *haecceitas*, of the concrete instance. For him the significance of particulars is cryptic; it must be "spelt from sibyl's leaves." In the poem of that title, "thoughts against thoughts in groans grind." We must be "ware" of the world because the "stained veined variety" turns into "black, white," as the "hornlight" of "evening" becomes "night."

The drama of knowing generally a world which floods us with particularity is seldom permitted in Hopkins' poetry to get resolved. "Praise Him," because "things" are "dappled." "His beauty is past change." And yet it is the contradictoriness, the singularity, the scantiness, the outlandishness, of things, that Hopkins names as the objects of God's "fathering-forth":

All things counter, original, spare, strange;[27]

This drama of knowing hovers over "The Windhover," which cannot be read classically as a statement, via several ambiguities, of a metaphoric identity between Christ and a kestrel. The sestet "buckles" under this usual interpretation of the poem, because Christ's "fire" is said by Hopkins to be phenomenally greater than, not in any sense equivalent to, the visual apprehension of the bird that he has dramatically recounted in the octave:

> Brute beauty and valour and act, oh, air, pride, plume, here
> Buckle! AND the fire that breaks from thee then, a billion
> Times told lovelier, more dangerous, O my chevalier!
> No wonder of it: sheer plod makes plough down sillion
> Shine, and blue-bleak embers, ah my dear,
> Fall, gall themselves, and gash gold-vermillion.[28]

"AND" is capitalized to do a coupling which does not hold even through the line, because "then" is needed to draw the logical conclusion. The surprising tonal fall of the last three lines draws two further, disjunct conclusions, anticlimatic instances which return the viewing person to the earth of plows and falling embers after he has risen to the billion-fold loveliness of the chevalier. In the light of the poem's movement, all the hyperbole of the opening tropes about the kestrel, which verge at times on the theology of the Son ("dauphin") provides no continuous metaphor about Christ. The distinction between Christ and hawk, not the similarity, is what allows the capitalized theological conclusion of "AND" to draw some connection between earth and heaven—some connection, but not the firm stipulations of medieval analogy that Marshall McLuhan[29] reads into the poem. The dramatic difficulty of connection, the search for connection, allows the "I" of the poem to rise in his opening emotional flight of euphuistic naming; this surge of feeling is possible in the

flush of excitement that accompanies what "I" "caught," because
the catch is a special moment, not an ordinary experience:

> I caught this morning morning's minion, king-
> dom of daylight's dauphin, dapple-dawn-drawn Falcon,
>   in his riding. . .

If these metaphors, "minion," "kingdom," "dauphin," held more
than momentarily, there would be no further place for the poem to
go. As it is, they collapse under the intellectual task; they are finally
said to "buckle." Collapsing and gathering, the ambiguity of "buckle"
focuses the poem in a dramatic process, but not in an intellectual
formulation. For the mind this experience comes to finality in the
semi-abstractions that buckle "brute beauty and valour and act,
oh, air, pride, plume"; and—or rather AND—in the cancelling conclusion of Christ that has buckled (brought together/made collapse)
the semi-abstractions.

The mind and the heart ("in hiding") transcend themselves in
the mystery of a devotion to Christ that exhibits an encompassing
generality (the living bird of the air, the slow plow, the burning coal)
by itself transcending the God-mirroring inscaped particulars of
sensory experience.

The obligations of the priest preserve the centrality of God; and
still the experience of the sensitive man who precedes the poet, the
Hopkins of the Notebooks, urges the particulars upon the poet. The
drama of devout human knowing takes place in the tension between
the "fire" of God and the shining that "leaps out" in the particulars
of the world.

Hopkins refurbishes a Victorian vocabulary with radical Saxon-
isms: then he subjects the words to a syntax-wrenching associativeness which is governed by his rhythmic flow much as his insight is governed by particulars. The tension of the poem's dramatic movement
contains a generality greater than either theological summary (the
beauty of the world proves God) or delectation over particular

sensibilia (blown bird, shining plow, gold-vermillion ember). Even under his strenuous concern for keeping the universal at the heart of a poem's affirmation, Hopkins' "instress" on particulars enlivens his intuition. The book stays open.

"The poet," Reverdy says, "is a giant who passes effortlessly through the hole of a needle, and at the same time a dwarf who fills the universe."[30] The modern poet writes about the universe as though it were a needle, a needle as though it were the universe. Such poets do not renounce universality; they come at it through particulars. If they really did abandon universals and universality, wholly, then their poems would close on some partial pastoral contentment, one of negation; or else on the limited contentment implied in the self-attributed scientifistic ignorance of "The Flower in the Crannied Wall."

A set meter, even in a poetic convention where set meters are fully dominant, seems to be putting the things named into an order additional to the order of syntax. When the syntax itself offers diffusion instead of coherence, along with a generality resistant to set designations; and when meters other than set ones exist as an attractive option for conveying perceptive openness; then a set meter, if it is chosen, seems to be insisting the more on its own order. The particulars yoke violently by harmony; and in the set meters of the *Sonnets to Orpheus* the violence and the harmony themselves come in for comment, while the meters, uniform in being set, are varied as though to declare the arbitrariness of the particular pattern, and therefore the equivalence of all patterns. In "classical" rhymed verse the rhymes themselves offer an ideological patterning as well as a rhythmic one, but the rhymes in the set meters of Pasternak's poems present junctions only cryptic, and there are no ideological patterns to be found in their pairings. He marshalls his particulars into quatrains where a heavy feminine ending regularly alternates with the close of a final masculine syllable.

These particulars, again, veritably breathe with a hidden significance:

> Full was the wood of precise scintillations
> As under the tweezers of a clockmaker.

Here, in his vivid particulars, the former graduate student of philosophy makes his philosophical studies the bridge to a description of his poetic process:

> . . . And it was in this gazing back that what is called inspiration consisted. The more turgid, uncreative portions of existence were realized with particular vividness, in view of the great distance of their ebb. Inanimate objects acted even more powerfully.[31]

Minutiae constituted reality, but in a kind of paradox that made objects more "vivid" as they became less lively ("inanimate"). He goes on, in this theorizing reminiscence, to speak of the general as moving when it is still ("the moving whole"):

> These were the living models of still-life, a medium particularly endearing to artists. Piling up in the furthest reaches of the living universe and appearing in immobility, they gave a most complete understanding of its *moving whole, like any boundary which strikes us as a contrast.* [Italics mine.] Their position marked a frontier beyond which surprise and sympathy had nothing to do. There science worked in search of the atomic components of reality.

> But as there was no second universe whence one could lift reality from the first, taking it roughly by the fore-lock, it was necessary for the manipulations which it incited, to take its symbol in the way algebra does. . .

The "manipulations" of fixed rhythms and free particulars, then, may move around the geographical world in an attempt not to depict it, but rather to adumbrate the "second universe" for which the perceptible world itself is furnished with particular "algebraic" symbols such as the Sphinx:

> Stars raced headlong. .
> > Thoughts raced headlong.
> To Sahara Sphinx turned patient ears . . .
>
> Seas were stirred by breezes from Morocco.
> Simoon blew. Archangel snored in snows.
> Candles guttered. First text of the Prophet
> Dried, and on the Ganges dawn arose.[32]

What is happening in this poem transcends its central events, the genesis of a poem by Pushkin and, diffusely, the rising of the sun over India.

Yeats' rhythms roughen as he comes under the compulsion to sound general, to gather more into the poems than the poems can hold, "the balloon of the mind" in a "narrow shed," "the uncontrollable mystery on the bestial floor." Nature and history exceed the ecstasy that would fuse them: "A shudder in the loins engenders there/the broken wall, the burning roof and tower." The poems stir and burst by trying to get the covering generality of A Vision into the turbulent instances of human life and nature. Let mystery be accepted, let it be hailed; and pat stanzas move into the generality of the oracular, where dream-like "Fragments" sum up an unspecifiable significance:

> Locke sank into a swoon;
> The Garden died;
> God took the spinning-jenny
> Out of his side.[33]

Here the Industrial Revolution happens in Eden, yet somehow the Expulsion precedes Eve.

Soberly rational, Mallarmé manages a tight conscious control over his diversities not only by his regularity of rhythm but also by inten-

sifying and generalizing the subject of the poem that he keeps seemingly closed on itself. More than the sky breaks out wildly into its
own identity in the conclusion of:

> *Je suis hanté.* L'Azur! l'Azur! l'Azur! l'Azur![34]

Between the italics of "I am haunted," and the hypostatizing capi-
talization of "Azur" works the turbulence to which the repetitions
and the exclamation points testify. The "azur," coming first in lower
case, overwhelms him already with its serene irony in the first line;
and he calls it eternal:

> De l'éternel azur la sereine ironie
> Accable,

Montale in "Lungomare" brings the pressure of his words' connotations to bear on a generality by enlisting only their denotations for
the narrative of the poem. Mallarmé, in a syntax of severely rational
progression, produces a comparable pressure by the opposite means:
he enlists connotations so severely that no denotation, or even alternate denotations, can emerge:

> Dis si je ne suis pas joyeux
> Tonnerre et rubis aux moyeux
> De voir en l'air que ce feu troue
>
> Avec des royaumes épars
> Comme mourir pourpre la roue
> Du seul vespéral de mes chars.[35]

> Say if I am not joyous
> Thunder and rubies at the axles
> To see in the air this fire pierces
>
> Amid scattered realms
> As though dying purple the wheel
> Of my sole chariot of evening.

This lies beyond the deliberately rapt diffusions of Eliot's imitation:

> Garlic and sapphires in the mud
> Clot the bedded axle tree.[36]

It also lies beyond the alternate denotations which Charles Mauron provides, because it offers no foothold in its generality for any such specific series of events, "a promenade in a carriage with wheels either actually red or merely reddened by the setting sun," or else " 'Thunder'. . . suggests thundering of a chariot . . . and explosion of . . . joy" or else "a show of fireworks."[37] In its indeterminacy the poem is quite unlike "The Ode on a Grecian Urn" or "The Good Morrow"—or even "The Sunflower." One might take for its series of events Mauron's sunset, his chariot, his fireworks display. But one could equally well read it as designating the progress of a declining king (sparse kingdoms, die, purple, chariot). Or of Zeus (thunder). Or the poet writing this very poem (at sunset; as a king, as Zeus, etc.). Such constructs do not constitute interpretations; they are linkages of connotations in some way attractive to the interpreter, but contrary to the firm generality of the poem.* It would be equally legitimate to quote these lines and apply them, say, to an automobile, as Proust[38] has Marcel do for a car he has given Albertine. The poem's achievement of high abstraction consists precisely in pitching its connotations to the point where such linkages of connotation cannot close the openness of its generality. To put it differently, as he himself might have put it, he enlists the plenitude of individual *words* (the famous remark to Degas) for an almost impossible fullness of designation. This of course involves "purity," or even "absence" of meaning. But such an absence, in Mallarmé's dictum, is inseparable from the highest generality of speech:

> I say: a flower! and, aside from the oblivion into which my voice relegates every contour, insofar as it is something other than the known calices, there arises musically,—the very idea and soft, the absent one of all bouquets.

> Je dis: une fleur! et, hors de l'oubli où ma voix relègue aucun contour, en tant que quelque chose d'autre que les calices sus,

---

*Mauron in his later work interprets recurring words in Mallarmé like "fire" as partaking of networks (*réseaux*) of relationship. Such networks imply a generality of reference for the poem; and in fact require some notion of generality to give them a bearing on the poem's signification.

musicalement se lève, idée même et suave, l'absente de tous bouquets.[39]

The generality of the word "flower" occurs when, and because, the special contours and known calices of rose or iris or daisy have been relegated into "the absent," whose fresh emergence from the act of saying forbids its becoming a substantive. We have "l'absente," and not "l'absence," or "la fleur absente." The result, in the word, and in the poem, is an idea in the Platonic sense, a self-identified intensity ("même") which produces a calm pleasure ("suave").* In the paragraph just before this one, Mallarmé affirms, by a rhetorical question, that the "marvel" of the disappearance of the concrete must take place before the word's "pure notion" can emanate from it:

> A quoi bon la merveille de transposer un fait de nature en sa presque disparition vibratoire selon le jeu de la parole, cependant; si ce n'est pour qu'en émane, sans la gêne d'un proche ou concret rappel, la notion pure?[40]

This vibrant suspension of an ideal generality of words from "the embarrassment of a near or concrete reference," can be sustained even in the concrete circumstance of a poem written for a given occasion, here the death of Théophile Gautier ("Toast Funèbre"):

> O de notre bonheur, toi, le fatal emblème!
>
> Salut de la démence et libation blême,
> Ne crois pas qu'au magique espoir du corridor
> J'offre ma coupe vide où souffre un monstre d'or![41]
>
> O you, fatal emblem of our happiness!
>
> Health of madness and pallid libation,
> Do not think that to the corridor's magic hope
> I offer my empty cup where a gold monster suffers!

*These modifications of *idée* came to Mallarmé in the final afterthought of revision; his initial version stressed loftiness and a more exuberant pleasure "(idée rieuse ou altière.")

Having "toi" refer to Theophile Gautier does not bring the poem closer to any specific reason why he is the emblem of our happiness, and a fatal one: we have either a *carpe diem* in the presence of a dead friend, or some statement about him so rich in its generality that the particulars of his life, and ours, are triumphantly bypassed, as the exclamation point helps to assert. And also identified. The identity is underscored by the rich, identical rhymes that prevail through the poem.

If *our* happiness, then who are we? The poem "answers" this question in another rich identity, "We are/the sad opacity of our future spectres." And this is announced by the haggard crowd (of mourners, of cosmopolites, of mourners as cosmopolites, of men in their "false pride," all men, or some, or these):

> Cette foule hagarde! elle annonce: Nous sommes
> La triste opacité de nos spectres futurs.

The syntax enlists, as it happens, also a (simpler) ambiguity of Empson's sort: do not think it is to the magic hope that I offer my empty cup/do not think I offer my empty cup to the corridor/do not think the cup I offer to magic hope is empty.

Since we cannot tell whether an actual cup is empty or not (or whether the cup is a real one raised in funeral toast, a metaphor for Gautier's "libation," or a metaphor for this "emptied" poem, "Toast Funèbre"), we cannot call the monster of gold that "suffers" inside the cup a yellow wine, or light, or an illusion of the poet's eyes, or a mythological figure chased into the metal of the cup, or the poet's idea (or any of these expanded correlatively into various metaphorical possibilities). At this funeral occasion, syntax levitates connotation into a transfixed meditation on the general human condition. The commonplace of *memento mori*, which forms the substratum of the poem, resolves no mysteries: it poses them. Ancient death rises, and with it a solid tomb where avaricious silence and massive night rest with all that harms:

> Surgisse . . .
> Le sépulcre solide où gît tout ce qui nuit,
> Et l'avare silence et la massive nuit.

"All that harms": is identical with silence and night, or else it is one of a series with them. The syntax moves "*et*" both ways, in a final generality. The funeral finalities ring off cryptically on one of Mallarmé's favorite rhythmic touches, the identical rhyme of a noun with a verb.

All poems set up connections, through syntax and rhythm, among the particulars they name. Among the initial connections a conflict of contradiction—the extreme of diffusion—can be set up to suggest the possibility of still other connections. The program of Surrealism tries to make such a conflict explicit by presenting logical contradiction in the procession of images:

> Je t'aime à la face des mers
> Rouge comme l'oeuf quand il est vert.[42]

These conflicts, further, are supposed to enlist emotions deep enough to have emerged from the unconscious, which is celebrated not, so to speak, for its own sake, but for its power to generalize diversities. Breton gives up his medical practise when he becomes a poet, and it is as a poet that he is received, somewhat coolly, by Freud. Here the emotions reside in the connotations of single words ("oeuf," "rouge," "mers").

Such conflicts appear with an accelerated frequency here, in one of Empson's kinds of ambiguity:

> O Thou steeled Cognizance whose leap commits
> The agile precincts of the lark's return;
> Within whose lariat sweep encinctured sing
> In single chrysalis the many twain,[43]

The double oxymoron (single-twain; many-twain) by which Hart Crane brings this invocation to a head, itself caps a series of tortuous conflicts "encinctured" in the metaphors that are broken through, and broken through again: from steel to leap, leap to bird, bird to lasso, lasso to song, song to chrysalis. The energy of change, which mpels these breaking metaphors, can be felt as pulling together the "tension" Tate finds in this passage. That is exactly Crane's poetic point: the God behind the bridge shows an energy, here verbally manifested as the words "break down," that dissuades us from taking this passage just for what it also is, a series of euphuistic riddle-like tropes for "bridge." God is neither merely immanent in the bridge ("Cognizance") nor merely transcendent ("leap"). Crane agonizedly celebrates a hoped-for but contradictory general unity; this, when it emerged from the chrysalis where it is by definition bound, would somehow fully unify immanence and transcendence. The Cognizance must be steeled, and also leap. Words embody cognizance, and they break down under it, as their extensions in metaphor break:

Of stars Thou art the stitch and stallion glow.

A certain heavy-handedness ("Thou art") and a contradiction ("stitch," "stallion glow") press the words till they bow down to a Oneness their praise asserts to be beyond them.

Or conflicts may be harnessed into a general equivalence. This is the practice of Dylan Thomas who speaks of a poem's "womb of war" and "warring images":*

*"A poem by Cameron *needs* no more than one image; it moves around one idea, from one logical point to another, making a full circle. A poem by myself *needs* a host of images, because its centre is a host of images. I make one image —though "make" is not the word. I let, perhaps, an image be "made" emotionally in me and then apply to it what intellectual and critical forces I possess—, let it breed another, let that image contradict the first, make, of the third image bred out of the other two together, a fourth contradictory image, and let them all, within my imposed formal limits, conflict. Each image holds within it the seed of its own destruction, and my dialectical method, as I understand it, is a constant building up and breaking down of the images that come out of the central seed, which is itself destructive and constructive at the same time. . . .
. . . the *life* in any poem of mine cannot move concentrically round a central image; the life must come out of the centre: an image must be born and die in another; and any sequence of my images must be a sequence of creations, recreations, destructions, contradictions. I cannot, either—as Cameron does, and as others do, and this primarily explains his and their writing round the central image—make a poem out of a single, motivating experience. I believe in the simple thread of action through a poem, but that is an intellectual thing aimed at lucidity through narrative. My object is, as you say, conventionally to "get

'Rest beyond choice in the dust-appointed grain,
At the breast stored with seas. No return
Through the waves of the fat streets nor the skeleton's
                              thin ways.
The grave and my calm body are shut to your coming as stone,
And the endless beginning of prodigies suffers open.'[45]

Birth? Sex? Death? The ambiguous conflicts of any one reading suggest the others, though the poem began, Thomas tells us, as a poem about birth. Again, these are not "alternate" interpretations in a usual sense. The sign-system of the poem does not first point at just "birth" or "sex" or "death," as "The Sunflower" first points at a flower or "Ode to a Nightingale" at a bird out a window. If "breast stored with seas" be taken for the beloved (seas: coursing blood) or the mother (seas: milk), its syntactic correlation with "in the dust-appointed grain" poses the conflicting simultaneous possibility of death. The poet celebrates, in trauma and in joy, the generality of human existence, an ever renewed religious miracle ("endless beginning of prodigies") which must be immolated ("suffers") to be realized ("open"). Not birth alone, or sex, or death, focuses the poem, but an opening pain whose generality includes all three, not as summation but as equivalent aspects. The language proclaims, in effect, their equivalence as the stigmata of their vivid authenticity: we know death by sex, birth by death. The three great events of a life merge in a general and mysterious suffered event that archetypifies them all.

A generality underlying birth, sex, and death is also presented in *Finnegans Wake*. There the multifarious specific conflicts of the statements are overridden by the slackening of a long narrative and the inclusiveness of a cosmic perspective. The death (of Finnegan), the sex act (of HCE and ALP), and the birth (of their children: of Finnegan, who rises at his own funeral)—all these are interwoven.

---

things straight." Out of the inevitable conflict of images—inevitable, because of the creative, recreative, destructive, and contradictory nature of the motivating centre, the womb of war—I try to make that momentary peace which is a poem.[44]

The circularity of the tale, its multiple identifications, the dream drift of syntax, the implosion of individual words, project birth, sex, and death onto a scale that allows their generality, in turn, to inter-lock with that of human history (primitive society to civilized, in the four Viconian stages) and of divine (the garden of Eden). The novel is not a personal testament, or an epic of civilization, or a disquisition on original sin, or a joke against scholasticism, or a poem about marriage, or a melting of language back into the flow of dream, "abnihilisation of the etym."* Finnegans Wake is remark-able not for being several kinds of book at once, but for being a unified book which not only uses these several kinds, as designated part to implied whole, but interlocks them in such a way that each is equivalent to the other (civilization to Eden, personal testament to original sin, poem about marriage to joke against scholasticism via a personal testament about original sin in Viconian perspective, etc.).

Designation gets lost in implication. The coordinates have been suspended by which we can tell the tale from metaphor about the tale, the manifest content of Finnegan's dream from its latent con-tent. Leaving that point aside (to be resumed protractedly in an-other chapter), we may still find in every sentence the force that has stirred sequence into a whirlpool of circularity, the pressure that has melted words into the dream-semblables of other words in the same or another tongue. The portmanteau words carry an ambiguous baggage of multiple meanings: these ambiguities are "inside" the portmanteau; there remains still the outside, the strange luggage by which we recognize this traveller. System, even the elaborate "epi-phany" system of correspondence (time, place, Homeric myth) in Ulysses, has been suspended, and the words are free to respond to the surrounding pressures. Multiple meanings alone could not create such a generality; the way in which the multiple meanings are asso-

---

*"Abnihilisation of the Etym" means the annihilation of the verbal root (etumon), but also the revocation of substance (atom), the abrogation of logical categories like "therefore" (et [en] im).

ciated retains the openness and arbitrariness that lets the idea of 'heaven" be read in every brick of this tower of Babel.

Merleau-Ponty's idea of the self-transcendence of language applies with special aptness to *Finnegans Wake*. "Let us admit as a fundamental fact of expression," he says, "*a bypassing of the signifier by the thing signified which it is the special property of the signifier to render possible.*" [Italics Merleau-Ponty's.] *Admettons comme fait fondamental de l'expression un dépassement du signifiant par le signifié que c'est la vertu même du signifiant de rendre possible.*)[46] Words are signs: they denote things, and they connote subsidiary others. But words are defective signs when they advertise their own defectiveness; when this happens, Merleau-Ponty is saying, the words have taken their own defectiveness into account. How does one then make words (a tale, *Finnegans Wake*) signify the universe? By making them specially significant, and also specially defective: the portmanteau packing of multiple significance, and the dream distortion of defective, "sleep-broken" communication, become one. Beneath the cryptic pullulations lies the principle of pullulation, the *Wake*. Which is, in turn, itself cryptic. Where does one ultimately turn? The signs do not point, they have lifted the distinction between denotation and connotation, not to abandon both for a kind of Lettrism or Dadaism, but to intensify both into an inclusive generality.

Beckett, one of the earliest to provide a theoretical setting for *Finnegans Wake (Our Exagmination)*, achieves a similar generality by suspending the distinction between denotation and connotation in ordinary language. Where *Finnegans Wake* has several tales that blur, the trilogy ending (perhaps) with *The Unnamable* has one tale that will not come clear. Does the trilogy constitute an expression, or an attempt to express? "There is no use indicting words, they are no shoddier than what they peddle."

> This time, then once more I think, then perhaps a last time, then I think it'll be over, with the world too. Premonition of the last but one but one. All grows dim. A little more

and you'll go blind. It's in the head. It doesn't work any more, it says, I don't work anymore. You go dumb as well and sounds fade. The threshold scarcely crossed that's how it is. It's the head. It must have had enough. So that you say, I'll manage this time, then nothing more. You are hard set to formulate this thought, for it is one, in a sense. Then you try to pay attention, to consider with attention all those dim things, saying to yourself, laboriously, It's my fault. Fault? That was the word. But what fault? It's not goodbye, and what magic in those dim things to which it will be time enough, when next they pass, to say goodbye.[47]

The "writer" here tries to take stock, or dramatizes the trying in taking stock. "Trying," "taking stock" are themselves aspects, not ultimates. The ultimate is a general condition towards which these words all point. Denotation serves for connotation, and vice versa. Words like "dim," "blind," "dumb," "fault," "magic," do not denote "absence of dark" or "deprivation of sight," or "absence of hearing," or "guilt," or "suspension of the laws of nature," nor do they connote "obscure," "imperceptive," "oblivious," "causal unrelation," "liveliness." They do both; they connote and they denote. Or rather, in doing both, they point beyond both, like *Finnegans Wake*, to a generality of experience where "you"—the writer's self addressing himself objectively—merges with "you," the reader addressed by the writer; and with "you," the generalized person.

In such a world, even paradox does not celebrate itself:

> The bleating grew faint because the sheep were less anxious, or because they were further away, or because my hearing was worse than a moment before, which would surprise me, for my hearing is still very good . . . .[48]

Paradox here crops up just like any other incidence of defective language, to be bypassed unostentatiously. Self and other, self and world, blur like any other distinctions:

> And the confines of my room, of my bed, of my body, are as remote from me as were those of my region, in the days of my splendour. And the cycle continues, joltingly, of flight and

bivouac, in an Egypt without bounds, without infant, without mother.[49]

The tale is—provisionally ("perhaps")—not many in one and one in many, but both many and one at the same time:

> And I am perhaps confusing several different occasions, and different times, deep down, and deep down is my dwelling, oh not deepest down, somewhere between the mud and the scum. And perhaps it was A one day at one place, then C another at another, then a third the rock and I, and so on for the other components, the cows, the sky, the sea, the mountains. I can't believe it. No, I will not lie, I can easily conceive it. No matter, no matter, let us go on, as if all arose from one and the same weariness. . .[50]

Multiple meanings alone do not orient a work toward such generalities. The hesitations of Beckett's Malone get confounded with his intuitions in the clear progress of this narrative, which uses abstractions ("components") and words of heavy romantic connotation ("sky," "sea," "mountains") but no discernible Empsonian[51] ambiguities.

One could not, again, get Empson's "seven types" of themselves to produce Mallarmé's kind of generality, or Marianne Moore's, because his types are special instances of diction and syntax in works whose central coordinates do not match such overriding simultaneities. This is just why ambiguities seem striking in the kind of work where Empson finds them: they are bursts of richness, momentary assertions which couple, one way or another, denotations from two classes of meaning. To point up the difference between Mallarmé's generality and the ambiguities Empson classifies, we may take one of Empson's examples: Pope's "sleeps in Port," includes wine (a member of a class of soporific drink) and harbor (a member of a class of places where one is not travelling):

> Where Bentley late tempestuous wont to sport
> In troubled waters, but now sleeps in Port.[52]

The ambiguity of "Port" connects these two classes: to be drunk means to be inactive in the seas of criticism; Bentley is both. But the classes do not stay connected beyond this point in the poem: *The Dunciad* does not continue to connect these particular two classes; nor does it produce the sort of generality which implies such connection. It is a very specific satire, and a satiric bite inheres in this phrase, "sleeps in Port," just because the connection between classes is a momentary one.

Beckett, on the other hand, offers us no classes: he questions the very nature of class words as he uses them, of language as he uses language. The generality of his vision is called into play in the vibrancy between questioning and the insufficiency of the very terms that must be employed in questioning. So the arch concentration of Marianne Moore on the chambered nautilus, of Ponge on the cigarette, provides a means of avoiding classes so as to avoid the subordination, the series of sets, which they imply: they aim not only to be literal and specific, but also to be more general than a framework of classes will permit, whether or not such a framework is jointed with ambiguities.

Even without ambiguities, multiple meanings may clamp down hard onto experience and still not create Mallarmé's sense of suspended statement or Montale's denotations, hovering with things unsaid. Robert Lowell repeatedly breaks into metaphor, away from Montale's spareness, in translating him. Here, in a poem of his own, he makes an elected figure (city's geography equals country's history) double with another (physical winter equals sterility of corporate elective choice) for a poem whose satire is savagely specific:

INAUGURATION DAY: JANUARY 1953

The snow had buried Stuyvesant.
The subways drummed the vaults. I heard
the El's green girders charge on Third,
Manhattan's truss of adamant,
that groaned in ermine, slummed on want . . . .

Cyclonic zero of the Word,
God of our armies, who interred
Cold Harbor's blue immortals, Grant!
Horseman, your sword is in the groove!
Ice, ice. Our wheels no longer move;
Look, the fixed stars, all just alike
as lack-land atoms, split apart,
and the Republic summons Ike,
the mausoleum in her heart.[53]

No ambiguities here (except possibly "in the groove," jazz slang combined with physical description). The multiple meanings converge into satiric pressure, and the double, or triple metaphor is brought to bear on a single target. The severity of the statement is enhanced by the tightness of the form, a sonnet unbroken between octave and sestet. The blunt stabs of the short, regular tetrameter lines gain added emphasis from the rhymes. "Want" here is a class word, and the images of stars and atoms suggest a total (unacceptable) order moving toward disorder. Multiplicity intensifies indignation: there is so much to say against the subject that it necessitates double references, an effect not unlike that of prose satire, Swift:

Your inherent portion of dirt does not fail of acquisitions,
by sweepings exhaled from below; and one insect furnishes
you with a share of poison to destroy another.[54]

The classical "bee" thus accuses the modern "spider," successively of thieving materials, valuing refuse, and turning his borrowings into the venom of hostility, all functions simultaneously proceeding from his spiderly nature.

Or Karl Kraus:

Denn er würde nicht Erkenntnisse bergen, nur den Schrecken des Wiedererkennens: das im Angsttraum einer Kulturverwesung Geschaute, der Alpdruck in Schwarzweissrot, das pressende Phantom aus Papier und Blut, ersteht wieder zu tödlichster Lebendigkeit.[55]

For it [a Nazi form of expression] would not cover up cognitions, only the fright of recognition; something seen in the anxiety dream of a cultural decay, the nightmare in black-red-white, the pressing phantom of paper and blood, subsists once again in deadliest liveliness.

The terror ("Schrecken") of his own prophecy ("Die Dritte Walpurgisnacht," 1933) makes his savagery ride over the distinction between dream and waking. Naziism is a nightmare ("Alpdrucken") which uses printing presses for propaganda ("druck; aus Papier"); and it also murders ("aus Blut"): hence the appropriateness (black and white for printed paper, red for blood) of its frightening colors, merged as in dream, black-white-red. "Alpdruck" fuses the printing press with the nightmare; as well as, perhaps, the penchant of the Nazis for a Nietzschean mountain mystique. Kraus is also saying that the Nazis heap up a mountain of print, an "Alpdruck." The freedom with which he weds these associations in his satiric flights reminds us of *Finnegans Wake*, but only from time to time. He is actually as specific as Swift, and does not score, except by remote implication, any other class of objects than Nazis.

One can, like Aristophanes, address several classes simultaneously, and still not approach the generality of Joyce or Mallarmé. In *The Frogs*, Aristophanes has Aeschylus cap sample Euripidean prologues with the phrase "lost his little bottle of oil." The character Dionysus listens, present in the play because he is the god whose statue is present at the festival. He responds like an Athenian groundling, too, especially when Euripides begins a prologue that refers to himself as a god:

EURIPIDES: Dionysus, who clad in thirsuses
              And the hides of fauns in the pines below Parnassus
              Leaps dancing . . .
AESCHYLUS: Lost his little bottle.
DIONYSUS: Alas I am struck again by the little bottle.

The words of Dionysus echo—and so themselves parody—Agamemnons' speech as he is murdered in the *Agamemnon* of Aeschylus. It is with the inconsiderateness, as well as the impulsiveness, of a groundling, that he parodies Aeschylus in the act of trying to support him. He is "struck" by the bottle as a spectator, but struck by Aeschylus' implied insult of capping lines about himself, the god Dionysus. The references here do not focus on a single target. They are multiple and helter-skelter; Greek gods, Greek heroes (Agamemnon), old fashioned playwright, new playwright, current Athenian society. The multiple references come to a head now and then, as all these do in the single line which Dionysus speaks. But the diverse ones here, like the concentrated ones of Karl Kraus, still create no generality. They include just the (many) references, and no more.

A simpler poem of Ezra Pound illustrates a greater generality than the more complicated Lowell and Swift, Kraus and Aristophanes:

THE GYPSY

"Est-ce que vous avez vu des autres—des camarades—avec des singes ou des ours?"

A Stray Gipsy—A.D. 1912

That was the top of the walk, when he said:
"Have you seen any others, any of our lot,
With apes or bears?"
　—A brown upstanding fellow
Not like the half-castes,
　　up on the wet road near Clermont.
The wind came, and the rain,
And mist clotted about the trees in the valley,
And I'd the long ways behind me,
　　gray Arles and Biaucaire,
And he said, "Have you seen any of our lot?"
I'd seen a lot of his lot . . .
　　ever since Rhodez,
Coming down from the fair
　　of St. John,
With caravans, but never an ape or a bear.[56]

Donald Davie, who sees some of the openness in this poem as well as the sharp directness of its diction, stops short of asking how generally the openness permits us to take the anecdote it presents:

> Pound's last cadence, "but never an ape or a bear," throws an oblique ray in just the same way [as Wordsworth's "Stepping Westward"], mingling with the predominant emotion a feeling, this time, of wistfulness, even frustration. A very similar arc of feeling is followed in both poems, but by Pound with a far finer economy. And undoubtedly Pound's is a musical syntax, where Wordsworth's is not. For consider: who is "up on the wet road near Clermont?" The authentic Romanies? Or the half-castes with whom they must not be confused. Or the poet himself, and the man he has encountered? We do not know, and it does not matter. For all that is required at this moment in the poem is the "up" and the "on," the release, like the call of a horn, into distance and altitude. Or when was it that "the wind came, and the rain?" Was it when he saw the half-castes, or when he saw the full-blooded gypsies, or in between his meeting either of these and his meeting with the man who addressed him, or finally, did the squall come while he and the man were ,talking? And again, it doesn't matter. This is a rattle on the percussion as the other was a call of the horn; syntax has become music.[57]

But no, this is not musical syntax, even in Davie's sense; what he notices is, rather, just in the diction, a Mallarmean generality of unspecified reference, achieved in a language simpler than Mallarmé's. In the face of this diction, heavily connotative because it resists denotation, we cannot, with Davie, specify the emotion of the poem as "a wistfulness at the heart of the wanderlust." The muffled joke of the end, the speaking poet's matter-of-factness, forbid our dissolving the poem into the specific emotion (wistfulness) that Davie may choose to hear (and we may not) in the general connotation of the suspended wind and rain, mist clotted in trees, gray Arles and "Biaucaire."* These images, like the social role and

---

*Here, as in the quotation, I follow Pound's archaic spelling and possibly deliberate inconsistencies.

physical look of the gypsy, are ideograms for which the lexicon is not given. The disjunction and openness of this little separate and inconclusive anecdote already look ahead to the adaptive polyphony of the *Cantos*. These words are as denotative as Montale's and as ripe with "unused" connotation (St. John, Arles, half-caste). But the denotations, as Davie reminds us, do not really function conclusively either. They throw us back on the connotations: how are we to take the ape and the bear: anecdotally, emblematically, like a *Bestiary*, like Aesop? We are left with a complex image, or else an interlocking series of images: an ideogram. (We cannot even say, to carry Davie further, that this gypsy has, or has not, an ape or a bear of his own.)

Since the anecdote does not conclude, each line adds something new that wears the double face of completion and of afterthought:

> With apes or bears?"

The speaker then rings the change of negation, an article and a singular, on his own completion and afterthought, the only repetition within the poem:

> . . . but never an ape or a bear.

To explain the singular we move back to the plural, back to both by way of alternate translation for the poem's French epigraph. There is no end to this. There is not meant to be. Yet the effect, emotional and visual and intellectual, remains sharp and clear. The trees are visible (nameable) in which the mist is clotted. Yet no Montale nature-mystique is offered, but only the specific experience, calling in its openness for a generality it does not provide. Clarity, not connection—participation, not classification—are sought, and exemplified.

One could list the "types" of generality as Empson lists the types of ambiguity: the generality suggested by the single instance of a happening (Montale) or an object (Ponge, Moore): the generality of unspecified reference (Mallarmé): the generality of interlocking experiences, sex and birth and death in Dylan Thomas. No critical purpose would be served by such a classification, because these generalities interest us only as they may be seen in individual works. Or, to put it differently, the types alone would tell us nothing. We want to know if a generality appears in the work and what it does there, not how we might want to classify it. Pound's generality in "The Gypsies" works and feels differently from Mallarmé's generality, "of the same type," (the unspecified reference), and both are different from the large, inclusive sweep in Perse's open books. What are winds in "Vents"? Physical currents of air, but metaphorical breaths of change, neither being a primary vehicle to the other's secondary tenor. And seas both exemplify and create fertilities and cultures, in cities and floods and poems about them: seas are at once "seamarks" and "non-seas," "Amers":

> Et vous, Mers, qui lisiez dans de plus vastes songes,[58]

He begins,

> And you, Seas, who have read in vaster dreams.

Vaster, that is, than this poem about the sea, than words, than human dreams, but some kind of words: "Lisiez."

Perse's poem advertises its own openness in the length of its cadences, the freedom and backwash of its connections. In a sense the poem is diffuse (like the sea), and yet the subject itself is so large that new elements do not constitute digressions. The savored particularities give the effect of merging with their object in a "live embrace," but the object is not the sea only, in the sense that the sea is Marianne Moore's object in "A Grave." Civilization, Word, Creative Force, Nature—these are all evoked, named. Named and praised, in the litany that the cumulative invocations of the poem recall, the rite of celebration it mentions again and again, a dream of a rite in which the word is all—poetry to acompany the march of a recitation in honor of the sea.

> Poésie pour accompagner la marche d'une récitation en l'honneur de la Mer.[59]

Here Mallarmé has been simplified without infidelity. His method is shown to be as adaptable for exuberance as it is for austerity. Perse sounds, too, the prophetic note, loud and clear: Rimbaud has been diluted, and also expanded. The "alchemy of the word" has become a formula.

Rimbaud's own intensities in *Saison en Enfer* mirror an act of the verbal will, one that makes the history of the West his own history, and makes a statement of universal sinfulness the starting point of a study of inevitable happiness:

> O saisons, ô châteaux!
> Quelle âme est sans défauts?
>
> J'ai fait la magique étude
> Du bonheur, qu'aucun n'élude.[60]
>
> O seasons, O castles!
> What soul is without defects?
>
> I have made the magic study
> Of happiness no one escapes.

Exclamation, question, assertion: in the open generality of simple statements, these become pure modes. The verse is so simple that it could be taken for a folk song—if its designations touched ground at any point. The speaker ("Je"), who is another ("Je est un autre"), cannot be said to see (or not to see) a seasonal landscape or a castle. To apply Sartre's point about this poem (*Situations* II), the exclamation is not a eureka, or a sigh, or even a refrain (though the poem develops it into one; it is given twice again in the fourteen short couplets). Rather, the exclamation is a mode which includes these, and which doubles a mode of syntax against the mode of the purely connotative diction (season, castle, magic, happiness, soul). Nature and Art (season, castle)? Castle in a spring or autumnal morning landscape? Nature as a defect of the soul? Art as a defect of the soul? The soul as failing nature in its defect? As failing art? As failing to preserve the castle? As unable to preserve the castle because civilizations pass and "il faut être absolument moderne"? This visionary poem stands at its calm height above the possibilities that it itself suggests. It evokes these ultimates without the platitude of Mallarmé (beautiful sunset, toast to a dead friend). "I wrote of silences and nights," Rimbaud has said (it is all recounted in the past). "I noted the inexpressible. I fixed vertigos":

> J'écrivais des silences, des nuits, je notais
> l'inexprimable. Je fixais des vertiges.[61]

The richness and urgency of this voice is powerful enough to have proliferated a wilderness of legend about itself, a wilderness mapped by Etiemble (*Le Mythe de Rimbaud*). The legends turn the poems into scriptures, which they pretend to be, and are open to. But they only pretend, and they are open to more than any specific theology of poetic vision could enclose. One could accommodate them with the *Sonnets to Orpheus*, that theology of poetic vision; and something would be left over, the urgency of Rimbaud's record. This is a season in hell, not a Rilkean season among castles.

Trakl, who writes as though he had digested the *Sonnets to Orpheus*, does not refer to a myth, but invents an aura of his own: "Helian," "Sebastian." Without either Rilke's doctrine or Rimbaud's stated program of vision, his generality appears through an openness of reference in simple, concrete sentences.

His naming and praising open into a slow mystery which steeps itself in the visual appearance of nature. Often Trakl uses color words, but bringing all of his color words together will never produce even such a color symbolism as Rimbaud's vowel sonnet cryptically suggests. The colors are on or off; blue or bluish, green or greenish, red or reddish or rosy:

> Die Hände rühren das Alter bläulicher Wasser[62]

> The hands stir the age of bluish waters.

In this poem ("Helian") the waters, which have been white, are to be black, which the walls are to be (they have been yellow and red also, and will be "full of leprosy", which may include white in its suggestions). And not only the walls: "November-destruction" is black too, and rooms, and finally mouths. Black offers its own off-shades, several times: brown, dark, shadowy. The walls (once black) are "full of leprosy," and "lepers mirror themselves in black waters,"

> In schwarzen Wassern spiegeln sich Aussätzige;[63]

"Let the song also remember the boy," he says, toward the end, ". . . the faded one who opens bluish his eyes,"

> Des Verwesten, der bläulich die Augen aufschlägt.[64]

Helian, "the sunny one," gets still another blue:

> Der stille Gott die blauen Lider über ihn senkt.[65]

> The still God sinks his blue lids over him.

Of a line from "Sommersneige" (Summer's decline),

> Gedächte ein blaues Wild seines Pfads. . .[66]

> A blue deer remembered his path. . .

Heidegger asks, "Whose paths are they that 'a blue deer' might remember? 'Remember' means 'to take thought of something forgotten.'. . . To what degree ought 'a blue deer' to think of that which is going under? Does the deer get its blue from the 'blue' that 'spiritually glimmers', and when night goes? . . ."[67] But Heidegger's last quotation is from still another poem, "Frühling der Seele" ("Spring of the Soul")—

> Geistlich dämmert
> Bläue über dem verhauenen Wald und es läutet—

> spiritually glimmers
> Blue over the hacked-down forest, and there rings—

Heidegger goes on to ring the changes on blue, and on darkness, with quotations from several other poems, getting no closer to the blueness of the deer in "Sommersneige." Nor could he ever do so, though he does develop some remarkably deep and challenging ideas along the way. He knows this, he has said as much in a preceding essay:

> What is this naming? Does it hang on just the known, representable objects and processes: snow, bell, window, fall, ring —with the words of a language? No. The naming does not distribute titles, does not employ words but invokes the word. The naming invokes. The invocation brings that which is invoked nearer. Still, bringing nearer does not thereby shape the thing invoked, in order to deposit it in the closest region of that which is present and so to dispose of it. The call does call hither. And so it brings the presence of that which before was uninvoked into a nearness. But while the call calls hither, it has already called to the thing called. Whence? Into the distance, in which the thing called abides as something that is still absent.

> Was ist dieses Nennen? Behängt es nur die vorstellbaren, bekannten Gegenstände und Vorgänge: Schnee, Glocke, Fenster, fallen, läuten—mit den Wörtern einer Sprache? Nein. Das Nennen verteilt nicht Titel, verwendet nicht Wörter, sondern ruft ins Wort. Das Nennen ruft. Das Rufen bringt sein Gerufenes näher. Gleichwohl schafft dies Näherbringen das Gerufene nicht herbei, um es im nächsten Bezirk des Anwesenden abzusetzen und darin unterzubringen. Der Ruf ruft zwar her. So bringt er das Anwesen des vordem Ungerufenen in eine Nähe. Allein, indem der Ruf herruft, hat er dem Gerufenen schon zugerufen. Wohin? In die Ferne, in der Gerufenes weilt als noch Abwesendes.[68]

If Heidegger ends here with his own interesting notions, he begins with a response to Trakl, who uses words as if he had been nurtured on Rilke's conclusion about speech in the *Elegies:*

> Aber später,
> unter den Sternen, was solls: *die* sind *besser* unsäglich.
> Bringt doch der Wanderer auch vom Hange des Bergrands
> nicht eine Hand voll Erde ins Tal, die Allen unsägliche, sondern

ein erworbenes Wort, reines, den gelben und blaun
Enzian. Sind wir vielleicht *hier*, um zu sagen: Haus,
Brücke, Brunnen, Tor, Krug, Obstbaum, Fenster,——[69]

> But later
> under the stars what should it be: *they* are *better* unsayable.
> So the wanderer brings, too, from the mountain rim's overhang
> not a handful of earth to the valley, all things unsayable, but
> an achieved word, pure, the yellow and blue
> gentian. We are perhaps *here* in order to say: house,
> bridge, well, gate, jug, fruit tree, window . . . .

In the brilliant polyphony of "Helian," Trakl presents his words as
though saying them did the whole poetic work, just as he does in
the near monody of "die Sonne," whose simple declarative sentences
recall the alphabet book as easily as they do the Bible (Abel and the
mighty hunter of Genesis seem to lie in the "darkness" behind the
third line):

DIE SONNE

Täglich kommt die gelbe Sonne über den Hügel.
Schön ist der Wald, das dunkle Tier,
Der Mensch: Jäger oder Hirt.

Rötlich steigt im grünen Weiher der Fisch.
Unter dem runden Himmel
Fährt der Fischer leise im blauen Kahn.

Langsam reift die Traube, das Korn.
Wenn sich stille der Tag neigt,
Ist ein Gutes und Böses bereitet.

Wenn es Nacht wird,
Hebt der Wanderer leise die schweren Lider;
Sonne aus finsterer Schlucht bricht.[70]

Daily comes the yellow sun over the hill.
Beautiful is the wood, the dark beast,
Man: hunter or shepherd.

Reddish rises the fish in the green pond.
Under the round heaven
The fisher travels lightly in the blue boat.

Slowly ripens the grape, the wheat.
As the day, still, declines,
A good and evil is readied.

As it becomes night
The wanderer lightly lifts his heavy lids;
Sun breaks from a sombre gulf.

What is an abverb? The beginnings of the first three stanzas pose
the question. What is a verb? Every line but the third and fifth has
one, and no more than one. What is color? We have three, one
almost redundant (the sun is always yellow), one perceptive (green
water is vividly seen), one strange (boats are not usually blue, but the
heaven is—which here gets no color word). No changes are rung on
these, but changes are rung on the adverbs, once by repetition in a
different position: "leise"; and once by positional echo: "täglich,"
"rötlich." And changes are rung on the words for darkness, "dunkel"
of the beast, "finster" (a "poetic" word) of the gulf.

What is a substantive? We get mostly these, two in every line but
the lines where night and day are named. One kind of substantive
has others classified under it: man, hunter, herdsman. And are fisher
and wanderer coordinated with man (all men are wanderers), or
subordinate (fisher, wanderer, hunter, herdsman)? These substan-
tives alone consistently get no adjectives at all, and the first line
without any adjectives at all (or any abverbs either) is the one that
names three straight off:

Der Mensch: Jäger oder Hirt.

This is also the only line that offers the logical possibility—an advanced one for this poem's language—of alternation: "or."

The severe simplicity, the deliberate innocence, of this poem,
thrusts these merely grammatical questions into the foreground.
They become the alphabet of the mystery that Heidegger's provisional formulations probe—with the indispensable help of Trakl's
verses. The world is so simple, the sentences say; and so easy to walk
out into, and so full when it is named, and so impenetrable behind

its veil. The last line, like a chord after a series of single notes, suddenly thrusts on the verbal threshold the possibility of a world to which inner and outer, subject and object, are meaningful but not final categories: "Sonne aus finsterer Schlucht bricht." As in the *Sonnets to Orpheus* we are not allowed to say this is just an inner sun (we are told of the outer one in the first line) or an outer (how could any but an inner one break from a dark abyss when it is night?). The article has dropped off, "Sonne." "Sun breaks," and this is the world.

"Poems are not made with ideas," Mallarmé is supposed to have said to Degas, "They are made with words." To make poems with words, as Mallarmé did, leaves the ideas that reside lexically in the words open for generality, for a plenitude of Idea rather than an absence of ideas. Trakl's poem achieves this plenitude without looking in the least like one by Mallarmé. Or by Rilke. If the openness of the *Sonnets to Orpheus* points one way toward Trakl, it points, as an abstraction, another way toward the poet whom Rilke translated in his last years, Valéry.

The *Sonnets* and the poems of Trakl show as much concern with the process of knowing (in the poems, the individual words that stand and combine) as with what is known (the "idea" of the poem). Valéry as a critic elevates this concern to an abstract principle, whereby the poem is a stage in the process of knowing as well as a self-consistent machine of words. ". . . I give to the will and to the calculations of the *doer* (*agent*)," he says, "an importance which I withdraw from the *work*."[71] [Italics Valéry's.] And we may say of his syntactical and rhythmic traceries of thought process, especially in "La Jeune Parque" and the "Narcisse" poems, what he said of Mallarmé, "One could say that he put the Word not at the beginning but at the end of all things."

The "speaker" in "La Jeune Parque" utters series of abstractions which Valéry might have uttered of his own philosophical processes. We know, in fact, by Valéry's account, that this was the genesis of the poem: he wrote several abstract lines before the figure of the Young Fate emerged.

A young Fate is active because she is a Fate, but passive because she suffers what happens; being a Fate, she is perceptive; but she is just coming aware of things because she is young. Erotic as a woman, she is impersonal as a god, and one can translate all her erotic impulses before the "serpent" into movements of fatality. "La Jeune Parque" presents a generality in which erotic impulses, fate, youth, and emotions (she weeps or hears weeping at the outset), and thought processes (the poem is "her" process of thought) are all subsumed under the generality of an existence that tries to understand them by putatively connecting them. Or, from another point of view, all those aspects are located in a being whose existence is thought of as including them all, and whose general language, therefore, may refer to all:

L'immense grappe brille à ma soif de désastres.[72]

The immense grape-cluster shines in my thirst of disasters.

The grape cluster may designate something erotic, the breasts of her supine nubility. Or it may designate emotions and be the tears she has been speaking of all along. It may be the stars she opened with, which may be part of her in turn: there is the hidden pun on *astre-désastre*, especially as stars, in a Fate's words, are linked with Fate. The previous line had spoken of such a linkage in the first person:

Je scintille, liée à ce ciel inconnu . . .

I scintillate, linked to this unknown sky . . .

The cluster of grapes may be nothing so visual as tears or stars or breasts, but itself a metaphor for the fate processes (with which those in turn are linked). The statement is cryptic, even orphic, in its generality: a Fate is speaking, is thinking along the open line of a process Valéry creates. The generality here is "classic," harnessing intellectual connotations rather than the romantic emotional ones of Trakl.

Here we have, on Valéry's own showing, an extension of Mallarmé's practise: the procedure of ending with the Word instead of beginning with it. Valéry made this remark about Mallarmé with reference to "Un Coup de Dés." And in that poem itself, to apply to it the statement that runs through it in bold capitals, a throw of the dice can never abolish chance: a specific interpretation of the poem can never supplant the hazard of fortuitous other combinations of the associations in the words, opened further by printing them sprinkled across the page so that the white spaces, as Mallarmé says, become themselves parts of the poem. And why not? The poem is as open as the white spaces. The white spaces withhold the dice that the words throw but leave, so to speak, blank of numbers. Or with algebraic symbols on them: "Abyss," "shipwreck," "feather," "master,"—these, in the abstractness of the sentences that refer to them, may play several roles, may figure in several interlocking tales. There is no thought process—we are given no "I"—and all the statements are already "there," deployed up and down in a fortuitous order on the space of the page. We furnish the thought processes, and they are open enough to lead to ideas as inclusive as those in *Finnegans Wake:* This is what Robert Greer Cohn asserts of "Un Coup de Dés," and the open structure, the syntax, of the poem, will support his assertion.

Valéry, for T. S. Eliot *(From Poe to Valéry)*, closes a full circle of the "pure poetry" which strongly and characteristically exhibits some form of the generality I have been discussing. Eliot looks for a poet to supplant the "pure" tradition, and I should like to conclude this chapter by examining generality in a poet who carries on as well as supplants the "pure" (or "symbolist") tradition, René Char. Exhaling the atmosphere of the Rimbaud seer-poet, Char is abstract enough to resemble Valéry's mind-poet, and yet the most immediately evident trait of his verse is a simplicity comparable to Trakl's. Generality has been digested by Char, as surrealism has been digested, and he achieves it not by forcing his statements in one of the many flamboyant ways I have considered, but by allowing a logical gap between image and image, or between statement and statement, or between one phrase and another in a single unit of syntax.

His handling of images produces cryptic junctions that extend the simple contrasts or alogic of the formulaic surrealism with which he began. The "simple" love poem, "Pleinement," enters into a common lyric subject, love and life (or death), but the "plenitude" of the title is somehow exceeded by the attributions of the poem. When it comes to deducing the connection of image with image, of image with abstraction, the reader is forced into an open world outside the poem:

Quand nos os eurent touché terre,
Croulant à travers nos visages,
Mon amour, rien ne fut fini.
Un amour frais vint dans un cri
Nous ranimer et nous reprendre.
Et si la chaleur s'était tue,
La chose qui continuait,
Opposée à la vie mourante,
A l'infini s'élaborait.
Ce que nous avions vue flotter
Bord à bord avec la douleur
Etait là comme dans un nid,
Et ses deux yeux nous unissaient
Dans un naissant consentement.
La mort n'avait pas grandi
Malgré des laines ruisselantes,
Et le bonheur pas commencé
A l'écoute de nos présences;
L'herbe était nue et piétinée.[73]

When our bones had touched ground,
Crumbling across our faces,
My love, nothing had finished.
A fresh love came in a cry
To revive us and take us back.
And if the heat had been stilled,
The thing that was going on,
Opposed to dying life,

Was worked out to infinity.
That which we had seen float
Edge to edge with sorrow
Was there as in a nest,
And its two eyes made us one
In a nascent consent.
Death had not increased
In spite of dripping wools,
And happiness not begun
Harking for our presences;
The grass was bare and trodden.

The "dripping wools" stand in logical, sequential relation to a time and place that offer other images—bones, ground, a cry, "that which we had seen float," a nest, grass. Yet we cannot bring "dripping" wools into the sets of relation that would alone close the meaning of the poem. If "death had not increased/ in spite of dripping wools," then a usual causal connection, here superseded, is posited between the two: dripping wools are usually followed by an increase of death, but not in this case. Emphasizing the present case, wool would have something to do with love, and with life: the richness of flocks of sheep, warm clothing, drenched pubic hair—these are all possibilities. One alternative could even be the botanical sense of "laine," the down on certain plants. Emphasizing the usual connection, the rain of spring on unshorn flocks, a dripping wool ought indeed to increase death. We could take the "death" side of the first possibilities (richness, clothing, hair, rain), or else import anthropological analogies from primitive tribes or the Bible (Gideon's fleece and its dripping wools). Death normally increases if wool is dripping, the poem has said, but not here because we have a "plenitude." Of life? (The lovers create life.) Of death? (Death cannot be increased when it has reached the state of "plenitude.")

The dripping of wool, then, might be an image for either life or death. It cannot simultaneously be an image for both, (except actively, a "dying life") in the plenitude of their paradoxical union, an experiential version, with Heraclitean echoes, of Rilke's death-in-life in the *Sonnets to Orpheus*. The simplicity of the images, the elusiveness of their connections, make this openness possible, but not necessary. The poem gives us a gap between dripping wools and death, and happiness, and grass, that we can never span.

Let the images be clear and the statements direct; Char may then create such a gap of openness between one statement and another, as in "Les Transparents":

<table>
<tr><td colspan="2" align="center">*Toquebiol*</td></tr>
<tr><td align="center">*L'habitant*</td><td align="center">*Inhabitant*</td></tr>
<tr><td>—Travaille, une ville naîtra</td><td>Work, a city will be born</td></tr>
<tr><td>Où chaque logis sera ton logis.</td><td>Where each house will be your house.</td></tr>
<tr><td></td><td></td></tr>
<tr><td align="center">*Toquebiol*</td><td align="center">*Toquebiol*</td></tr>
<tr><td>—Innocence, ton voeu finit</td><td>Innocence, your vow ends</td></tr>
<tr><td>Sur la faucille de mon pas.[74]</td><td>Upon the sickle of my step.</td></tr>
</table>

Toquebiol's answer provides the key: he gives the title to this section. It is not the habitant's "logis" that "ends"—the house similar to all those of his neighbors and to which he has entrée; it is his "voeu," wish or vow. Is the vow also the house? Does "innocence" designate the "habitant," include him, or have nothing to do with him? Work in the fields, beyond the French farm town of clustered identical houses, may take the sickle as tool. Does "faucille de mon pas," then, answer "Travaille," or ignore it? Multiple associations are possible from one "proverb" to another, but they cannot hold across the gap of their equally possible contradictions. At the same time the neat couplets summarize their speakers emblematically: the confrontation is as total as it is mysterious, even though mainly the habitant asks Toquebiol to be a townsman, and Toquebiol mainly answers that it is better to wander.

Char achieves this generality, without either cryptic image or obscure dramatic sequence, in the obscure but simple syntax of *Partage Formel* and *Feuillets d'Hypnos*. From one of the aphorisms in the former he takes the title of his comprehensive collection: *Fureur et Mystère:*

XIII

Fureur et mystère tour à tour le séduisirent et le consumèrent. Puis vint l'année qui acheva son agonie de saxifrage.[75]

Fury and mystery in turn seduced him and consumed him. Then came the year that completed his agony of saxifrage.

Leaving aside the serial implications of his Roman numerals (more formal than Arabic ones in the *Feuillets:* it is *Partage* Formel) we may see the "Transparents" gap between the first sentence and the second. But the syntax of the first sentence can itself be taken at least twelve different ways, depending on what kind of copula we make of each of the two "et's," and whether we read the central adverbial phrase ahead or backwards or both ways. This syntactic proliferation of Empsonian possibilities gains added force, of course, from the fact that all the words are highly connotative ones, both intellectually and emotionally. Again, the aphorism is too short, too open, to utilize the ambiguity for Empson's essentially ornamental purposes.

"Le Poème Pulverisé" does not abandon these techniques but advances them. It is the *poem* that is pulverized. So, in "Donnerbach Mühle," we have the three obscure generalities of image ("Pleinement"), sequence ("Toquebiol"), and syntax ("Partage") all at once.

Tracée par le canon,
—vivre, limite immense—
la maison dans la forêt s'est allumée:
Tonnerre, ruisseau, moulin.[76]

Traced by the cannon—
to live, immense limit—
the house in the forest is lighted up.
Thunder, brook, mill.

Apocalypse resides the more mysteriously in the last three images for their returning us, via a literal translation, to the German of the poem's title and the mill's name (Donner, bach, mühle). The name is "pulverized" from one German compound substantive into three separate nouns kept apart by commas. What is a title, what is a name? To have seen this mill, named in the enemy's language, while patrolling these woods for the idle French Army in Winter, 1939—the visual and personal side of the *image* only deepens its mystery (deliberately, because we know these details from the "notes" of Char's later appended "Arrière-Histoire"). And we cannot construct solutions by reference to *syntax*—the only syntax in this last line is a bare nominalization. Or by *sequence*—the dashes keep the sequence open, as does the immediate transition from the concrete "cannon" to the abstract verb "to live."

Yet this poem, for all its "immense limit" (more than the classical oxymoron "measureless thing-measured"), possesses the ultimate clarity of triumphant statement. The book stays open, the generality holds.

: III :

RHYTHM

In his poem's rhythm, as in other features of its statement, the "classical" poet adopts the stance of an expected poetic discourse, noticeably retaining that stance through the poem: the classical poet, that is, adopts the design of meter. Inside the formal framework of his verse design, set and pre-existent as it strikes the ear of a listener schooled in the conventions of its patterns, he creates the rhythm of his own poem, the overall sound of his individual verse instance and all the smaller verse instances that go to make it up.

The verse instance, in the variable flow of spoken sound, must necessarily vary somewhat from the verse design, the set pattern of meter and such other set patterns, rhyme, for example, that he may have chosen. Even if iambic pentameter does correspond to the predominantly binary structure of English phonetics, the language has four levels of stress accent, not two; and in addition to stress, the syllable has pitch and duration; the phrase has superfixed intonational patterns and conventional junctures.

Still, the verse instance may seem quite close to the verse design, as in the accentual-syllabic regularity of *The Faerie Queene*, where the pentameter has always five accented stresses and always ten syllables. None the less, not only over Spenser's smoothness, but also over the roughness of Donne or the latitudes of Shakespeare's dramatic verse alike, does the design remain dominant; and in all these cases, smooth and rough, we get a counterpointed interaction between verse design and verse instance. In the best analysis I know of, the metrical effects gained from such counterpointing; Arnold Stein[77] lists four categories of interaction between verse design and

74

verse instance (though he does not use this Jakobsonian terminology): "sound used (1) almost as an abstract vehicle, (2) as
naturalistic imitation, (3) as a contributing metaphor, (4) almost
as a complete metaphor." In all these categories, including the last
one, while the subtleties of metered verse can be analyzed, those of
freer modern verse cannot, because in modern poems the meter,
even when it is present, is not so firmly established as to constitute
a ground for the instances, and thereby to provide a "complete
metaphor." Stein's term, however vague it may be, cannot be made
to cover William Carlos Williams, or even Montale.

Even when the modern poet does choose meter to begin with, it
is as something more than Stein's "abstract vehicle" out of the set
staple of a necessary convention. The modern poet is free to choose
meter as one among several possibilities, much as a modern painter
might choose to be representational. Even the regular Valéry says
he hears the rhythm of the poem before he has any words (imply-
ing a unique rhythm for the large instance of the individual poem,
and not the conventional design of a set meter). And his meters are
abstractly regular to the point of seeming not a conventional stance
but rather some ratiocinative game invented on the spur of the
moment. "The exigencies of a strict prosody," he says, "are the arti-
fices which confer on natural language the qualities of a matter that
resists, alien to our soul and as though deaf to our desire."[78] This
negative definition of metrical design, which goes profoundly against
the grain of Sidney or Puttenham, implies the pre-eminence of the
verse instance. For one like Valéry who occasionally wrote verse in
free form or in prose, the strict meter had become no longer a stance
but rather an arbitrarily adopted "*matière résistante*," with no hint
of *musica mundana*. Moreover, Valéry speaks of the poetic art as an
improvisation even when it adopts a formally abstract music: "Pur-
suing an object that does not differ excessively from the one the
musician has in view . . . he must create or recreate at every instant
that which the other finds all made and ready to hand."

All the more does free verse get the poem's rhythm beyond any of the counterpointed and counterpoised interactions of design and instance. As Maritain puts it, "Modern poetry is bound to obey more exacting laws and rules, for they are free and contingent rules, depending at each moment on the correctness of the ear, and on the fact of each and every word, measure and period in the poem being exactly in tune with the soundless music stirred by poetic intuition within the soul."[79] (Still, the last half of his statement applies with equal force, though different relevance, to the classical poem that does counterpoint design and instance.) He goes on to quote Cocteau, "These mysterious rules are with regard to the old rules of versification what ten games of chess played at once are with regard to a game of dominoes."

In free verse, and more emphatically in the self-styled linearity of "projective verse," there is a weighted, and contingently posited identity, between an external linear unit of line or breath or syllable and the overall cadence of the instancing voice. Since no set pattern is stipulated, design does not emerge, and cannot stand fast for instance to be counterpointed against it. Convergence is substituted for interaction; an equivalent for design is produced in the modules of separable units, and the cumulative effect is reserved for the instances. That is, the principle of regularity is not cumulative, the way we recognize blank verse (or another design) after two or three accumulated lines. Instead of being cumulative, what here corresponds to design is unitary, since it is based on one variable line or on a variable syllable count or on the "breath" between two junctures or on some limit of syllables per line produced in process, or on some combination of these. Any given limit works within vague boundaries, those of the unit, and under rules that are fairly loose ("no more than double the number of syllables in the last unit, and no fewer than half," or some such). These rules are never so precisely formulable as those of a set design, blank verse or another. And because there is no cumulative "click" of the design, the units themselves are sequential, discrete, and linear, moving projectively ahead. To put it another way, design has been stretched to include

all features, potentially at least; pitch and juncture, as well as stress
and syllable-count, come in for attention, as all instances do, since
no pre-established rule of design emerges. All instances share in the
free-form pattern, and share equally to the extent that they are not
firmly ruled out. In blank verse, by contrast, a fixed caesural juncture
is firmly ruled out of the design, and so it is firmly instantial when it
occurs there. But in the design of the alexandrine, the caesura is
firmly ruled in. It must come after the sixth syllable of every line.
When Ezra Pound and Marianne Moore happen to use an alexandrine, though, we get not a sequential and cumulative regularity,
but a unique instance (an instance that at one moment, somewhat
ironically, "quotes" a design—that of the alexandrine).

The modern poet keeps the intimate voice of his rhythm open for
adaptation to the intuitive current. This openness allows even for
regularity as a possible conversion of its stance. Nothing in the prose-
poetry of "Donnerbach Mühle" prepares us for the sudden incursion
of regular meter in the last four lines:

> La lune du lac prend pied sur la plage où le doux feu
> végétal de l'été descend à la vague qui l'entraine vers un lit
> de profondes cendres.
>   Tracée par le canon,
>   —vivre, limite immense—
>   la maison dans la forêt s'est allumée:
>   Tonnerre, ruisseau, moulin.

The regularity reaches a near limit of design in the last line (as the
nominalizing syntax of the line sets a limit for parataxis): each word
is an exact iamb, and each one has the metrical foot set off by the
juncture which the commas indicate. The hexasyllabic trimeter (half
an alexandrine) is suddenly set in the first and second lines, but
broken in the third line, as though to insist on the momentariness of
these choices. Against that break, the overdominance of the trimeter
in the last line insists on the strength of the impetus to regularity.
The third line has eleven syllables, just short of the twelve that
would balance it against the first two; but also it has no caesura after

the sixth syllable, and so has not begun to suggest an alexandrine. Design here functions not as a counterpointed term, but as a momentary option.

This freedom from interaction between design and instance will hold all the way through a free verse poem, even when some sort of design has been arbitrarily assigned to the poem. William Carlos Williams chooses a measure that partially reproduces the *terza rima* of Dante while remaining quite free of Dante's marshalled counterpoint between instance and design, rhyme or meter. The *terza rima*, chosen perhaps for the Dantesque subject of praise of a beloved woman, sustains its verse instances through a series where no metrical design emerges because no two of the lines are metrically alike (except perhaps lines 5 and 14):

TO BE RECITED TO FLOSSIE
ON HER BIRTHDAY

Lèt hím whŏ mày
ămông thĕ cŏntínũĩng lìnes
séek òut

thàt tórtŭred cónstănĉy
àffiŕms
whère Ĩ pĕrsísted

lèt mĕ sáy
ăcross crôss púrposès
thăt thĕ flowĕr bloòmed

strúgglĩng tŏ ăssért ĩtself
símplŷ ùndĕr
thĕ cŏnflíctĩng lights

yoû wìll bĕliéve mĕ
ă róse
tŏ thĕ eńd ŏf time[80]

The terminal line of each of the last three triads produces an identical dipodic pattern, itself varied within the foot from the prevailing iambs. So, by the end, the rudiments of a pattern are felt as coming into being. But a design, again, cannot be established as an inflexible rule here, and the instances move simply and quietly through the syntax of three unpunctuated sentences, recitative ("to be recited") and intimately informal ("Flossie"). If in "The Desert Music" Williams produces a norm of three two-stressed phrases, if Yvor Winters finds a dimeter or trimeter norm in this or that poem, the norm is lost in its variations, the design in the instances. Never for a foot does the voice enlist itself into a fixed rhetoric of sound: it moves in its artful, uninsistent variations. This stillness, "rose-like" in its unfolding, pervades the poem, as the adaptiveness of the verse instances do not lose themselves in any "struggling" or "conflicting" of counterpoint against design. Each line unit is free of the "normal" metered or designed references to the other lines. Since we have not an indeterminate number of lines, but a *terza rima*, this freedom moves in an order observed on the page but not otherwise prescribed for the voice.

The pattern of pause, in fact, is primarily a syntactic one, and enlists sound only as syntax must. The line endings do not counterpoint their nascent design, by enjambment (except at line 11) or lack of it, against their instances. For the line, metric design converges with rhythmic instance; not a single pause of notable length occurs within one of these lines. Moreover, pause is formally marked here by lines, and only by lines: there are no punctuation marks.

When design is predominantly present in modern verse, it does not necessarily have instance set against it as repetition (design) against variation (instance). In Gottfried Benn's poetry the iambs, though recognizable, get submerged so easily that we cannot label them as design (repetition) or instance (variation). In this case the iamb cannot be called a rule of design or an instance of voice alone; it exists indeterminately suspended between both. Montale in his "blank verse" poems returns to the hendecasyllable as a norm, without enlisting the counterpoint between design and instance: the instances of hendecasyllable are so regular that they correspond quite closely to that design for the moment, and yet the other variations depart so far from it that the design does not emerge in the engulfing voice. In "A Liuba Che Parte," for example, the instances of the first three lines stir so forcefully that not till the fourth line, half-way through the poem, does the hendecasyllable noticeably appear and then it remains for re-use without ruling itself in as the poem's formal design:

1 Nòn ĭl grillŏ/mà ĭl gáttŏ
2 dĕl fòcŏlárĕ
3 ór tĭ cŏnsíglĭă,/spléndĭdò
4 lárĕ dĕllă dĭspérsă tŭă fămíglĭă.
5 Lă cásă chè tŭ réchĭ
6 cŏn té răvvóltă,/gábbĭă ŏ càpĕllíeră?
7 sòvrástă ĭ cĭechĭ témpĭ cómĕ ĭl flúttŏ
8 árcă lĕggéră/—ĕ básta ăl túŏ rĭscáttŏ.[81]

Not the cricket but the cat
of the hearth
may now advise you, splendid
house-god of your dispersed family.
The house you carry
wrapped up with you, is it birdcage or hatbox?
it stands over the blind times as a light ark would
over a flood—and is enough for your redemption.

Besides the (suspended) interaction between verse design and verse instance, there obtains in this poem, as in any, an interaction between its sound and its senses. Interaction between design and instance in a poem may or may not take definite place; interaction between sound and sense must: spoken words perforce have a sound, words perforce have a sense, and the mere fact that a group of words acts as a poem calls its sound into special play with its sense. The emphases of Montale's first three lines here overturn the design-instance interaction so powerfully that no design can emerge. Thereby the sound-sense interaction acts more nakedly, establishing itself as fully dominant in the poem.

Rhythm here, then, comes into being as a variable field of force governed only by the intermediate line endings. As the rhythm breaks over from the third line into the arbitrarily opted hendecasyllable of the fourth, it marks the line-ending by a strong enjambment, "splendido lare." Against the strong norm of the first three lines, with their differing lengths and accentual patterns, the design of the hendecasyllabic cannot appear more than as a momentary option of the line: a hendecasyllabic line, instead of setting up a dominant design, emerges as a single instance which happens to conform to a design, but momentarily. The short fifth line is thematically central, recalling by its shortness the first three lines; and by its regularity—it is the most regular of the eight—the iambic design of hendecasyllable. The single instances of arbitrary, not normative, design, vary among themselves: and the presence of design in the last three lines, remaining arbitrary against the bare, varied instances of the poem's opening, establishes more powerfully the sense of regularity, in the life of Liuba as in the statement of the poem. Regularity, in sound and in sense, cannot be taken for granted; it must emerge out of the transition from low design to high design, as Liuba must build up a new home out of one physical object clutched in her hand. The quiet balance of regularity is fleetingly suggested by the single incidence of a rhyme between the very last word in the poem and the last word of the first line, "gatto," "riscatto"; the only other rhyme insists on its character as instance by occurring internally, "consiglia," "famiglia"; by occurring between words which are equivalent just in termination, and neither in position nor by nature (one a verb, the other a noun). The strongest set of positional-natural equivalents spans the majority of the poem's statement, from the first line ("non il grillo ma il gatto") to the sixth ("gabbia o capelliera"). These two pairs of nouns, equivalent by syntactic correlation, by position, and by lexical association (the members of the first pair are both animals; of the second, containers) gain an added equivalence from the verse instance of dominating accentually the lines where they occur.

Hendecasyllable, rhyme, internal rhyme, caesura, positional and natural equivalences[82]—all these regular features of design move in and out of the poem, markedly but momentarily; design becomes instance, and sound adapts itself provisionally and intuitively to sense. This poem's rhythm produces the illusion of adhering nakedly to the contours of the speaking voice; it dons the clothing of design not as a woman might put on a ball gown but as a naked woman might drape a scarf over her neck. If she were painted she would thereby become a nude;—Montale's lines constitute, after all, a poem, and not a naked act of speech.

A poem can move more often than this into a set line and still suspend a commitment to design. Robert Lowell achieves the sense of a voice speaking directly and unrhetorically (*Life . . .*) in lines that approach fairly formal design (*Studies*):

1	Up in the air	M
2	by the lakeview window in the billiards-room	M
3	lurid in the doldrums of the sunset hour	M
4	my Great Aunt Sarah	F
5	was learning *Samson and Delilah*.	F
6	She thundered on the keyboard of her dummy piano	F
7	with gauze curtains like a boudoir table,	F
8	accordionlike yet soundless.	F
9	It had been bought to spare the nerves	M
10	of my Grandmother,	F
11	tone-deaf, quick as a cricket,	F
12	now needing a fourth for "Auction,"	F
13	and casting a thirsty eye	M
14	on Aunt Sarah, risen like the phoenix	F
15	from her bed of troublesome snacks and Tauchnitz classics.[83]	F

The normativeness of blank verse cannot prevail in these lines when almost half of them fall short of pentameter. Nor can normativeness of iambics prevail when either the slack syllables are heavily

syncopated as in lines 4 and 11, or else the stresses occur in a pro-
fusion that does not rise to the design of sprung rhythm. (For one
thing, in no line till the last are the many slacks sustained by the
"proper" number of five stresses.) Again, as in Montale's poem, the
unit of actual pause seems to determine the line length, especially
when there are no enjambments, or at best very weak ones.

Rhyme, too, serves as instance rather than as design. It occurs only
twice, and then weakly, once as an off-rhyme with an unrhymed line
in between (air-hour), once on the feminine endings of the two final
lines. Feminine endings come on ten of these fifteen lines, so often
that they cannot be taken for instances of variation on a standard
feature of English blank verse design, the masculine ending; but in-
frequently enough that they, in turn, do not lock the poem into a
design, especially when the first three lines of this verse-segment all
do have masculine endings, and when there are so many other variations from the iambic norm. This voice wears the iambic rhythm, so
to speak, as transparently as the gauze curtains on the Freudian
boudoir table. It speaks in obedience to something that is acknowledged: the motivations; and to something that at the same time is
not fully apparent: the unconscious. The pulsations of blank verse
move below the surface, acknowledged but unassertive, offering the
recurrences of design without providing the relief, and set form, of
a definite expectation. The structural implication of rhyme, like the
structural implication of psychoanalytic understanding, emerges as
a possibility in the instances of reported converse. To touch rhyme,
lightly, acknowledges the possibility. The voice is remembering, but
the memories are kept from being maudlin, or even nostalgic, by the
light undercurrent of regularity, an undercurrent that is never permitted to become the main current. The voice "free-associates" in
its rhythms as in its statements: though "free-association" is an artifice for the poem, a triumph in the poetic universe comparable to
that of uninhibited free-association in the psychoanalytic one. The
poem, of course, begins by "imitating" an analysand's recollections.

Still it is not a taped segment from actually speaking an analysand, nor is it the prose autobiography that Lowell began to write before he "discovered" a rhythmic possibility which uses Pound's phrasal rhythms in the direction of a feigned regularity recalling that of one of his favorite poets, Montale. (The feminine endings recall the hendecasyllables, of Dante as well as Montale; and Lowell is speaking of the long past, of the dead.)

A syllabic base for verse gives it a free ring by liberating it from a primary dependence on the foot. When the number of syllables is not quite constant in such verse, design tends to disappear. "Syllabic" is itself a misnomer when applied to Marianne Moore's verse, if it is meant to suggest some regularity of a metered sort but on a different base from that of stress. Her variation is too great, and it is accomplished, as Robert Beloof[84] points out, by too many other sorts of variation, to be more than a recurrent instance of verse; it is hence not a verse design, except in a few poems.

Even a short syllabic poem does not need much variation to submerge design. In this poem of Robert Creeley's, for example, there is a syllabic equivalence of sorts: 32 syllables divided over 4 lines, averaging 8 to a line. We have that average in the two middle lines, with one syllable more in the first line and one less in the last, creating a pattern of 9,8,8,7.:

FOR A FRIEND

Whŏ rĕmémbĕrs hìm álsŏ, hè thínks
(bŭt tó hĭmself / aňd ás hĭmsèlf).

Hĭmsélf / ălóne / ĭs dómĭnaǹt
ĭn ă wórld ŏf nó oǹe eľse.[85]

Here the "usual" accentual system, by contrast with the syllables, is powerfully varied. In a poem with so much instanced variation of stresses and slacks, so complex a syllabic "pattern" gets lost: it cannot emerge as a regular design against which the instances work.

It only hints at regularity, as the poem's statement only hints at identity. The hints of identity are broader in the other metrical features: the word "himself," repeated three times, gets a prepausal stressed downbeat each time, and the only other definite prepausal stressed downbeat ("world" is a possible one) comes after the word which modifies and isolates the last "himself," "alone." In metered verse, the prepausal stressed downbeat[86]—an instance (stressed) of accent at the point where it should come in the design (downbeat), heightened by a juncture (prepausal)—provides a marked convergence of instance and design. In the absence of firm design, as here, it is not so marked.

In Marianne Moore's own poetry, the design of syllabic recurrence is rarely applied with full regularity, and her "stanza" characteristically contains lines of such varied length that a movement of conversational ease is sustained. The syllabic design, itself varied, becomes a design only from stanza to stanza, not within an individual stanza. In their conversational ease, the instances of the individual lines predominate over the design of the complexly organized stanza. The echo from stanza to stanza has to be picked up across a number of lines, and then without more than an occasional instance of rhyme to heighten the suggestion of design. Her effect is not at all reminiscent of the strophes of Pindar and Bacchylides, which are also built not on a uniform line but on a repeated stanza. In their work a sense of regularity is reinforced by complicated syntax, and also by the (lost) musical accompaniment of flute or lyre. Marianne Moore's voice moves along, within the design of the syllabic stanza, as though improvisationally. The very casualness of the voice is liberated for its ruminative undertones by the syllables, which, in being counted for design, divest the accents of some of their own suggestion of design. As in Creeley's poem, the accents, by not receiving an expected patterning, and the syllable count, confuse each other. The accents, as random instances, strike the ear more lightly, especially when the line units themselves end on particles or on

PRISMS

enjambments that seem to relax the counterpoint rather than to heighten it, as enjambments usually do:

SPENSER'S IRELAND

No. Syllables
4	hăs nót áltečed; —
8	ă pláce ăs kínd ăs ĭt ĭs gréen,
8	thĕ gréenĕst plàce I've névĕr sèen.
7	Evĕrȳ náme ĭs ă túne.
9	Dĕnùncĭătĭŏns dŏ nòt ăfféct
7	thĕ cúlprĭt; nòr blóws, bùt ĭt
11	ìs tórtŭre tò hìm tŏ nót bĕ spóken tò.
4	Thĕy're nátŭràl, —
5-6	thĕ coát, lìke Vénŭs'
5	mántle línĕd wĭth stárs,
12	búttŏned clóse ăt tĕe nečk,—tĕe sleèves néw frŏm disúse.[87]

The syllabic design of this much-varied series of lines is followed in the next stanza, but not wholly in the third (that stanza ends with a syllable count in the last five lines of 6, 5, 9, 6, 12, the numbers of the varied lines being italicized). The couplet of the second and third lines is repeated throughout the poem, but within this first stanza it has the single instance of rhyme (a frequent practise in Marianne Moore's verse, the single rhyme set against the patterned syllables). The stanzas that follow do not, as this one does, contain an off-rhyme in the fourth line; and so "tune" after "green / seen" turns out to be an instance. Other off-rhymes (Venus', disuse), initial rhymes (to, tune) and assonance (to, tune, disuse) occur haphazardly, as light touches suggesting a pattern hidden in the cadenced movement of the lines.

The dashes, and the variation in clause length, make the voice seem halting. In their wide latitude, the instances of accented stresses do not pull against a prevailingly iambic norm, as in Montale and Lowell; the norm is not iambic but syllabic, and so the instances of stress do not insist emphatically. They come when they come, freely, without even a momentarily hinted counterpoint. The echo of Spenser's alexandrine at the end of every stanza contributes to the banter of the poem, a *trompe l'oeil* rhythmic reference to the title. The end line of *The Faerie Queene* stanza is reproduced, complete with medial caesura—but the medial caesura is not retained regularly (being dropped, in the third, fourth, and sixth of Moore's six stanzas). Feminine endings, and the special Moore touch of a feminine ending with strong enjambment, ("but it / is" "Venus' / mantle") keep accent from combining at all regularly with line-ending, thereby preventing the strong and overbalanced emergence of a simple line. The voice, cultivated with delicacy, values order as much as improvisation, design as much as instance, and manages a fine balance between them, moving simply past the possibility of strongly asserted interactions by producing other instances. The movement remains circular: stanzaic; and the thought ends where it began, without a classical stance being assumed at any point. The rhythms, like the animals of her poems, become not emblematic designs or naturally observed instances, but orderly manifestations of lively action.

Her line unit, even when it is not organized into the stanza, carries on its own interaction against the movement of the voice. The sense of unity in the line gains by not having the line submerged to a pattern of accents, as in "A Grave":

> Man looking into the sea,
> taking the view from those who have as much right
> to it as you have to it yourself.[88]

The first line here has seven syllables, the second twenty. I discern no closer pattern in this poem than the alternation of a line with many syllables and a line with somewhat, or far, fewer. Every line is an instance, every pair a lightly imbalanced set of instances, strengthened only once by an identical rhyme (look / look), once by an off-rhyme (them / foam), and once by a terminal word (or identical rhyme) repeated over an interval of seven lines, the title word, "grave."

The syllabic imbalance is only righted once, in the eighth of the eleven couplets: and the balance carries with it an added fillip of associativeness—these lines, with twenty-two syllables each, break the previous instanced limit for a line, twenty-one. Once the limiting case of syllabic balance, twenty-two and twenty-two, has been set for one couplet, the concluding couplets stay closer together, line by line and among themselves, than the opening ones did—except that the new provisional convention of breaking a limit is adhered to once again when the next-to-the-last line is given twenty-five syllables, three more than any line up to then. Imbalance, too, is reasserted: at this point there are six syllables of difference between the last two lines, twenty-five and nineteen respectively; when, after 22-22, we had 17-18, and 19-19. Twenty-five breaks the limit for the line, but it occurs in a couplet that adheres to the limit for the couplet: twenty-five plus nineteen exactly equals twenty-two plus twenty-two:

22   moving together like the feet of water-spiders as if there
                              were no such thing as death.
22   The wrinkles progress among themselves in a phalanx—beautiful
                              under networks of foam,
17   and fade breathlessly while the sea rustles in and out of the
                              seaweed;
18   the birds swim through the air to top speed, emitting catcalls
                              as heretofore—
19   the tortoise-shell scourges about the feet of the cliffs, in motion
                              beneath them;
19   and the ocean, under the pulsation of lighthouses and noise of bell-
                              buoys
25   advances as usual, looking as if it were not that ocean in which
                              dropped things are bound to sink—
19   in which if they turn and twist, it is neither with volition nor
                              consciousness.

The last word, "consciousness," resolves all the syllables by slowing its own down; by being the longest word in the line, and by constituting a series of three in long quantity, and by producing accents that seem to "hover" by staying on second and third degree stress (in the Trager-Smith system) rather than first and fourth. This slowing effect perhaps explains why Marianne Moore did not accept Ezra Pound's[89] suggestion of reversing the last two nouns. The syllables move, so to speak, like the wrinkles under the networks of foam in the sea she describes. Pattern is provisional, as metaphor in this poem is provisional. The voice remains orderly while (the lines are long) becoming breathless.

The syllable-count here varies too much to approximate a firm pattern. Rather, it works inside the limits of an improvised rule: 'No more than this number of syllables in a line and no fewer than that.' This important rule, which might be called the rule of the syllabic margin, has not been formulated by metricians. And yet it is to be found very widely exemplified in free verse, most notably in Whitman, who operates under the rule of the syllabic margin when he can be shown to operate under no other rule.

A boundary of silence, in the actual lineation of a syllabic-margin poem, gets demarcated when the syllables establish the margin as the limit of their field. Within that field, against that limit or up to it, their freedom—for combinations of stresses, pitches, junctures, and metrical arrangements of syllable groups within the line—is as wide as possible. Design under such a rule cannot be a ground against which instances are counterpointed when there is no case within the margin of the line itself of effects definitely ruled in, or definitely ruled out, the way metrical designs usually operate. The syllabic margin is, rather, a shaping boundary within which the instances can assert their free liveliness. Still, the boundary is there; we are not dealing with prose, or even with cadenced or "projective" verse.

In all these various practices, verse design has been subjugated, and verse instance becomes the new master of ceremonies. But one form of design remains, the line unit. To destroy that is the limiting act of a free verse: the prose poem of Baudelaire and Rimbaud, Mallarmé and Valéry.

The prose poem posits a poem of high formality: total design; and also of high informality—the unit of line and the unit of cadence, the syntax of a given statement and the arbitrary form of a poem, have become identical. The prose poem offers the zero case of divergence between instance and design.

The prose poem is not, of course, prose. A composer of music may destroy tone signatures and write an actual composition in which he scores together a thump on a washpot and a woman's screech. This highly formal act, by its context of definition, differs crucially from a washpot thump and woman's screech heard in accidentally conjoined sequence along a back street. Meter declares a formal context: the ritually poetic stance. A free poem declares that its context will only be that of the given poem. A prose poem bares its context of all reminiscences of meter: the act returns to formality through stark informality. (Much as an atonal composer might go through his work and obliterate all passages which recalled a given key-signature. Montale and Lowell, like Debussy, change the key-signature, so to speak, in mid-passage.) The prose poem is also the zero case of meter.

The effect of prose poetry is one of high deliberation, of exactly calibrated effects in the orbit of a freely moving "prose": and this is no paradox—every instance has now become a feature of design.

A still further heightening of this displayed convergence between design and instance comes about when the prose of the prose poem is stripped to the aphorism, René Char's practise in *Partage Formel* and *Feuillets d'Hypnos*. For exactly cadenced sentences, he substitutes the single aphoristic sentence. Or at best a pair of sentences. In this context, the rare longer passages seem to have their cadences muted. When one sentence can do so much—can stand, again and again, as the whole unit of a poem—then an individual sentence in a series of sentences sounds relatively unimportant.

Or prose poetry, free verse, and metered verse alternate as though indiscriminately, in "Donnerbach Mühle," "L'Araignée" of Ponge, *The Cantos*. The implied stipulation of rhythmic options in a modern poetic context differentiates these poems from the Menippean satires of antiquity. When the ancients mingled prose and verse, that form was set to begin with. A definite stretch of prose was followed by a definite stretch of verse. But the mingled meters of our poets do not contain units which must be sharply differentiated from other units (or must *not* be). The transitions are open, and so are the units.

In a modern poem even of formal design, if the design is broken in the right place, the whole tone can be made to change, and the voice to take on both softness and a sense of freedom. By disappointing some formal expectations, the effect of free verse can be counterfeited along with a designed pattern itself. So Hart Crane handles the design of the rhymed tetrameter quatrain:

> It was a kind// and northern face//
> That mingled in such exile guise//
> The everlasting eyes// of Pierrot//
> And, of Gargantua,// the laughter.
>
> His thoughts, delivered to me
> From the white coverlet and pillow,
> I see now, were inheritances—
> Delicate riders of the storm.[90]

Design depends on expectation, and when Crane disappoints expectation in the first stanza, he does so at points so crucial that he throws the whole poem into a different key. The entire rhythm rises lightly from the design when an internal rhyme (guise-eyes) anticipates the expected terminal rhyme of the quatrain (face, *-ace), which is then disappointed. The non-rhyme, pivoting on "Pierrot," gains another disappointment when the last word of the stanza— also unrhymed at the point of maximum expectation (but we now have learned to expect no rhyme)—rides over for a feminine ending, "laughter." More is at work, including a sudden overturning of stress regularity in the fourth line, upon the heavy stress-contrast and instance-insistence of "Gargantua." In these short lines a skillful variation of syllable lengths for words figures also: we do not expect a word as long as "everlasting"; and then a monosyllable, just ahead of the first crucial end-rhyme disappointment, fulfills an interior rhyme: "eyes." The next stanza changes the points of disappointment: the feminine ending comes already in the second line, "pillow."

These touches subvert the orotundity of an elegiac tone: they turn the rhythm of the poem into a stillness by making it seem to fall short of assertiveness: elegy becomes an undertone, the quiet thought about the dead friend that barely seems to drift its way into words.

Pound achieves a similar effect somewhat more formally in the "Medallion" that concludes "Hugh Selwyn Mauberley," by rhyming the stress of a masculine syllable with the slack of a feminine one:

> Honey-red, closing the face-oval
> A basket-work of braids which seem as if they were
> Spun in King Minos' hall
> From metal, or intractable amber;
>
> The face-oval beneath the glaze,
> Bright in its suave bounding-line, as
> Beneath half-watt rays.
> The eyes turn topaz.[91]

This is even more regular than Crane's poem. And still expectation is disappointed at the crucial instances of the rhyme words; in a reversed order, here, the first pair being slack-stress (oval, hall), the second pair stress-slack (were, amber). These irregularities are not permitted to become a design of their own; the next rhyme is a standard one (glaze, rays), and the next balances off-stress and off-stress (as, topaz). And the rhyme pairs are themselves in consonance with one another.

The lines, designed with respect to their prevailing iambic meter and in their rhymed quatrain grouping, stand as instances not only in the handling of rhyme but in the varied lengths of the sequence: here we have, in succession, tetrameter, hexameter, trimeter, pentameter, and then tetrameter, tetrameter—and, finally, two five-syllable lines that seem to hover between trimeter and dimeter. The hexameter line in the series possesses an even greater regularity by adhering to the medial caesura of conventional alexandrine design. The voice rises as though from amorous nostalgia in this longest line; but its instance turns out to be contained in the strict accentual-syllabic pattern. The design gives the poem the clear outline of a medallion; the instances, in their crucial management, do not flesh out the design but rather carry on their own transparent music of undertone.

Expectations even more multiple are turned loose in *The Cantos*, among prose sections, metered sections, and free-verse sections. The predominating free-verse sections, in their simple linear movements, deploy eclectic reminiscences of designs: blank verse lines, French syllabic lines, hendecasyllables, Greek dipodic units, common English measures like iamb and trochee, and less common ones that perhaps also recall the Greek. The reminiscences multiply, design submerges design, each turning the other into instance: as one *persona* submerges another in the adaptive singularity of the speaking poet's own voice. This, to begin with, overcomes the English heroic line, as John Berryman points out, quoting these lines from Canto LXXXII:

1   Swinburne my only miss
2   and I didn't know he'd been to sèe Lándòr
3   *and* thèy tóld me this that an' tôther
4   ănd whèn ôld Mátthèws wént hè sáw thĕ threê téacùps
5   twó fŏr Wàtts-Dúntŏn whŏ liked tŏ lét his téa coòl,
6   Sŏ old Élkĭn hàd ónlў óne glòrў
7   Hĕ díd cârrў Álgĕrnòn's súitcăse onc̀e
8   whĕn hè, Elkĭn, fírst càme tŏ Lóndŏn.
9   Bŭt gívĕn whàt I knôw nów I'd hàve
10 gót thròugh ĭt sómehòw . . . . Dírc̆e's shàde
11   ŏr ă bláck-jàck.

"Consider the opening dactyls here," Berryman says, "and then the spondee-two dactyls-and-trochee of the beautiful sixth line."[92] And the meters he hears are some of the many designs present in the submerging instances of this deliberative voice. Yet the metric foot, like all features of design, must be recognized by a norm the lines gradually establish, and what can the norm be here? The second, third, and fourth lines can be heard also as variations on an iambic (not a dactyllic) norm. The second line can also be taken as a hendecasyllabic (especially in a poem that imitates Dante and quotes Italian), or else as a blank verse line with a feminine ending. The third line, with its nine syllables, can be heard as syllabic verse; or, again, as iambic pentameter. The fourth line can be taken, among other possibilities, for exhibiting the design of alexandrine, complete with an exact count of twelve syllables and a medial caesura. Against these norms, one would hear the first line as instance-variations against a design of iambic trimeter, not as dactylic. And one could hear the sixth line not only in Berryman's dactylic design, but also against the design of blank verse, with a kind of choliambic ("limping iamb") substitution of trochee for iamb at the end in "glory" (with an echo of satirizing "glory," the classical function of choliambics).

Or, again, one can hear lines two, three, and four getting pulled into the dactyllic-spondaic orbit. And not only that; accordingly, Hugh Kenner states one possibility in the form of a denial: "this isn't one of the Greek meters salted with an abnormal proportion of long syllables;"[93]—but yes, it is that too.

Or, yet again, one can take the measure dipodically, as recalling Greek lyric strophes. The first line can be scanned as in logaedic measure, the sixth as built on a dactylo-epitritic base, the dipodic meter of Pindar. The phrase after the dots in lines ten and eleven is a perfect resolving glyconic, used, as in classical poetry, for its normal function of resolving a series of cyclic dactyls or pherecratics. If any one meter predominates, in fact, it is the cyclic dactyl, that varied staple of classical strophe. And the pivotal line five may be taken for a varied series of them, or the first half can be scanned as a dochmius. Greek meters allow, with the strength of a dipodic or larger base, for far greater variation of instance against design than do English meters. Taking such allowances, one could scan the whole passage here by using only classical dipodies: glyconics and pherecratics, cyclic dactyls, dochmii, and reizianums, etc.

These three mutual possibilities of design-scansion—Greek dipodies, or else iambs ("rising rhythm"), or else trochees and dactyls ("falling rhythm," with the stress first)—are not superimposed on each other, as sprung rhythm may be said to superimpose one meter upon another. They are not superimposed because they are only possibilities: no one emerges as a main design. Design of sound is only suggested, precisely as design of sense is only suggested in the overall coherent-diffuse organization of the poem. Instance here resolves into an interchangeable series of three (or more) designs— and there are more regular metrical passages elsewhere in the *Cantos* for further interchange, as well as occasionally the less regular passages of quoted letter or prose document. Along with, say, three possibilities over a whole passage, other momentary possibilities also occur (alexandrine in line four; choliambic in the terminal trochee-after-a-downbeat of lines two, three, four, and six). The effect is of great modulation (multiple design) and of great freedom (masterly instance), an effect comparable to that of prose poetry, where the instances are so diverse we attend to each one: instance becomes design. Or the poem slows down; as Kenner goes on to say: "its nature is to isolate *each* of the words so that we have not primarily 'lines' diversified with a pattern of stresses but a succession of unshakeable terms." Lines, however, are exactly what we do have: the movement of the line is the one unambiguous feature of design in this poem—as in most free verse, the line is the feature that permits all the other permutations of design and instance to take place. The "terms" seem to be suspended in an equilibrium of two or three gravities, two or three possible designs, all at once; and the rhythmic movement of the poem can be "slow" without losing any of its improvisatory freedom, at no point resembling the even slowness of a ritual procession. Syntax itself, to adapt Donald Davie's phrase, becomes music, because an underlying polyphony of dual and triple key signatures returns us to the syntax, to the cadences—as prose poetry does, but without the starkness of prose poetry.

Many musics still mingle in the unstopped ear of this Odysseus, and the words ride in their equilibrium along the doubled melodic lines, "unshakeable terms," in Kenner's phrase. Instance is not counterpointed against design, but design against design, so that instances multiply their effect through reciprocally-slowing designs. Because the voice is fluid, we move on—because it is retarded, we dwell on word and phrase, as Pound himself does:

> That leads out to San Piero. Eyes brown topaz,
> Brookwater over brown sand,
> The white hounds on the slope,
> Glide of water, lights, and the prore,
> Silver beaks out of night,
> Stone, bough over bough,
>   lamps fluid in water,
> Pine by the black trunk of its shadow
> And on hill black trunks of the shadow
> The trees melted in air.[94]

Since the design reminiscences move adaptively, the presence of an extra slack syllable may tip the design-possibilities not in one but in two or three directions. The definite article, then, functions not only as a delicate semantic alternative, but as an amplified rhythmic alternative. Without the article, bare nouns and monosyllabic adjectives produce stress syncopations: "eyes brown topaz, / Brookwater over brown sand." The third line sharpens the focus by adding the slack of "the" before each of its two nouns, and producing, among other possibilities, the momentary illusion of strong dipodic single design ($\smile''\smile\smile'$). The slight variation between the predominant bare stress nouns and the nouns with the definite article, between singular nouns (sand, slope) and plural (eyes, hounds), comes to a head in the pair of nine-syllable lines that recapitulate the two alternatives

—'with-or-without article' and 'singular-or-plural'—in a single instance: "the black trunk/ black trunks." One of these—necessarily—
has three syllables, the other two: but the shorter one is the plural.
Moreover, this difference is offset by a positional identity: adjective
and noun come both times at the fourth and fifth syllables, and each
line has nine syllables. So the first "trunk" rises out of the wood—
three syllables against nine—slightly more, in its cadence, than the
second "trunks" does. Audible alternation becomes, and serves, a
visual alternation, the precise image of the first line, and the precise
shift to the second. Another step and the sight is gone from the eyes:

> The trees melted in air.

If the two previous lines have an identical number of syllables,
this line in turn is identical with the line before them not only sylla-
bically but accentually too—except for one item, the definite article
on which so many changes have been rung:

> lamps fluid in wat ⌜er⌟
> ⌜The⌟ trees melted in air

The article picks up, so to speak, the overhanging slack in "water"
and puts it at the beginning of the line. Syntax resolves as music
resolves, and this sequence turns out, as we enter the next Canto,
to have been preparing for a music momentarily more formal in
its design:

> Compleynt, compleynt I hearde upon a day,[95]

which moves through its own variations to changes rung on a prose
quotation from a chronicle:

> And in August that year died Pope Alessandro Borgia
> *Il Papa mori.*[96]

A natural voice turns out to be echoing—or momentarily not, as it
chooses—a multitude of formal musics; so in *The Cantos* a conversa-

tional self-portrait conceals its instances of latent content in manifestations of selves and attitudes. Pound's rhythm, like his organization, is not eclectic in *The Cantos,* but syncretic, and the growing together of its constituents is made to seem audible in its very process of transformation.

: IV :

ALLEGORY

ALLEGORY, with a fixity by which we recognize it, represents something usually abstract (B) by something else usually concrete (A).
This is the root meaning of the word: by something else *(all-)* to
make a statement *(egoria)*. To recognize its fixity is easier than to
define allegory, one of the most ancient critical enterprises, perhaps
the one most directly connected with comprehensive philosophiz-
ing, from Plato through Philo to Porphyry. All sorts of shadings are
present in the form, as Graham Hough[97] insists in persuasively de-
tailing them. And critics from Coleridge to Northrop Frye have been
concerned both to establish its structural implications and to dis-
tinguish it from comparable structures (usually "symbolism"). As
Angus Fletcher[98] demonstrates, it may imply, or at least derive from,
an anthropological notion of "daimonic" possession; or it may suggest a larger cosmic order.

Of course literary works of other kinds may perform both of these
functions. But peculiar to allegory is the fixity by which a woman
(A) represents, say, Shame (B) or Chastity (C): something concrete
and visible stands for something abstract and unseen. In the simplest
cases, A carries the name of B:

> There was a womman eke that hight
> Shame, that, who can reken right,
> Trespas was hir fadir name,
> Hir moder Resoun; and thus was Shame
> Brought of these ilke twoo.
> And yitt hadde Trespas never adoo

99

With Resoun, ne never lay hir by,
He was so hidous and so ugly,
I mene, this that Trespas highte;
But Resoun conceived of a sighte
Shame, of that I spak aforn.
And whanne that Shame was thus born,
It was ordeyned that Chastite
Shulde of the roser lady be[99]

The allegorical function here is fully explicit, just a little more so than in Spenser, whose Chastity bears another name, Britomart. And that woman, as Hough points out, represents Chastity only intermittently. Still, when she does she does; A points at B. And however complex allegory gets, the initial fixity of structure remains the same. The Lucy and Matelda and Beatrice of the *Divine Comedy* possess not only a fourfold function but a richness of suggestibility transcending any quartet of abstract attributes. Still, we do have allegory; A stands for B, however complex B may be. When we pass to the Perdita and Marina of Shakespeare, though, we may still remain in the atmosphere of allegory, and allegorical suggestions may intensify those women and the events in which they are found, by which they are known; yet with all of this, the structure of allegory, the fixity of function that is its touchstone, is clearly absent. A no longer stands for B; Marina and Perdita are mainly themselves, however rich with significations (including quasi-allegorical ones) they may be.

Now a modern allegory, like Beckett's *Endgame*, does present something concrete on stage, A, which seems to be pointing instantly as the curtain rises at something abstract, a fixed B. Hamm and Clov are like Britomart, not like Perdita. Moreover, the things we see on stage are clear: we have a blind authoritarian who gives orders, just as at a point in Dante's *Inferno* we have a slow boatman who transports souls.

But—and this is the crucial difference—we can work out the something else that Charon anagogically stands for; Dante in the

Convivio and the letter to Can Grande provides a scheme for us to do so. Hamm, though, is indeterminate; he and his action, allegorical in framework, do not translate allegorically. The action contains its own generality in a way that other plays do not. Everyman in the medieval Morality stands at the point of his death; but which side of death, where in history, does Hamm stand? In *Hamlet* a highly complex but ultimately finite and specific series of events plays itself out. We are totally in Denmark. In *Endgame* we are not totally in a chess game, or in history (Sedan and the Ardennes are mentioned), or the Christian year (we hear of Christmas) or the family. The simple situation cries out for an interpretation the play thwarts by generalizing it. The cry cries out, too, against the thwarting. A simple stage set is given, either concrete (the inside of a tower) or abstract (the mind). The coordinate relations of Vladimir and Estragon in *Waiting for Godot*, and the subordinate relations of Lucky and Pozzo, have been worked into an equation with only two terms: Clov is subordinate to Hamm as his servant but coordinate as the man who can move. Coordination and subordination stand generally as a paradigm for all human relations, of which Hamm and Clov are fixed—but not specified—allegories.

Clov moves straight but captures any initiative at an angle: a pawn (or he is, to Hugh Kenner, a knight who hops—we do not have to choose). Hamm is a blind king, circumscribed to "one move" in any direction. In chess, the endgame may be defined as that point in the game beyond which the game may be thought of as a closed system, where all possible moves may be plotted, as they may not be plotted so exhaustively in the opening or the middle game. But what are the rules of this chess allegory? Who are the players on the other side? Who can capture Hamm? How is he to be checked or mated? Not by his parents, who are not pieces, but do occupy spaces, blocked or stalemated. Possibly Hamm is to be checked by Clov, who has seemed through the play to imitate the action of going away and striking out for his own independence.

Taken another way, this game cannot be imagined as ending when, as the play opens, it is called an infinite monotonous series:

> CLOV (fixed gaze, tonelessly):
> Finished, it's finished, nearly finished, it must be finished.
> (Pause.)
> Grain upon grain, one by one, and one day, suddenly, there's a heap, a little heap, the impossible heap.[100]

Or else the game makes contributions to something that materializes into definite shape, "a heap." And if Clov went away, what would be his game, when he has meaning only in relation to the king?

From the theatrical context we know that this game is comic. And satiric. Its action is to protest against itself. Prometheus appears here as Sisyphus, or vice versa. Even Clov has a mythical stature. Hamm is wider awake, when he comes awake, and also blind. His first speech has a different range, a more obsessive power (I omit the stage directions.):

> Me—
> —to play.
> Old stancher!
> Can there be misery—
> —loftier than mine? No doubt. Formerly. But now?
> My father?
> My mother?
> My . . . dog?
> Oh I am willing to believe they suffer as much as such creatures can suffer. But does that mean their sufferings equal mine? No doubt.
> No, all is a—
> —bsolute.
> the bigger a man is the fuller he is.
> And the emptier.
> Clov!
> No, alone.
> What dreams! Those forests!
> Enough, it's time it ended, in the shelter too.

> And yet I hesitate, I hesitate to . . . to end. Yes,
> there it is, it's time it ended and yet I hesitate to—
> —to end.
> God, I'm tired, I'd be better off in bed.[101]

The intense generalities of the statements and their sequences hold
Hamm's blind, dominant figure to an allegory of gesture. He is not
answering Clov, whom he has not heard; and so, on stage, his speech
must counterbalance Clov's, allegorically. The completeness of his
speech—from sleep to a rebeginning of sleep—makes it a summary
of the Human Condition. Hamm is not motivated, he is Motive.
He and Clov do not develop, they reveal, not by acting upon each
other, but by mixing, in the process of acting out feelings, an allegorical scheme of experience. This particular speech insists on persistence over despair, in despair, by its exclamation points. Similarly,
it proceeds to definition, and undermines definition, by perpetual
contradiction. The self-undermining general language is itself under-
mined by an inarticulateness that cannot swallow the words of
greatest urgency: "to—to end," "a—bsolute."

The scheme of this allegory keeps turning back to itself. In normal
allegory, on the other hand, one thing (A) stands for another (B).
The pigs (A) in *Animal Farm* are really men (B), embodying in
their allegory a classical metaphor: B is like A with respect to x, y, z
. . . Men are like pigs with respect to greed, selfishness, gregarious-
ness. Or in the Chaucer quotation above, Trespas has little com-
merce with her husband Resoun. So she must conceive Shame by
sight.

Allegorical interpretation of Scripture follows this model consistently, even in dealing with persons from earlier scriptural history.
St. Paul reads Hagar and Sarah (A) as revealing, respectively, the
bond life and the free (B). Without denying their personal existence, he does not return to it for interpretation, as one must do in
interpreting *Endgame*: Hamm (A) is Hamm, and to produce a
figure chess king or Superego or Prince of Players (Hugh Kenner's

suggestion: "Me . . . to play") gives us a new term, B, for which the significance itself becomes and returns to the original person, A, Hamm again.

We do not even arrive at a procedure comparable to the ones necessary with Beckett when we take the traditional allegorical reading of *The Song of Songs*—Solomon and his bride (A) figure Christ and his Church (B)—and enrich it by applying B to A as well: the Pauline idea that Christ and his Church (A') are the model for husband and wife (B'). (A) has become (B'), but we do not have to return to Solomon again. Solomon, in this reading of *The Song of Songs*, remains the vehicle, Christ the tenor. The separation between vehicle (A) and tenor (B) grows wider in the abstraction of medieval allegory—a Rose (A) being fulfilled love (B), or an armed maiden (A) being and acting elaborately as imprisoned or freed Chastity (B). And yet this equation tends to hold for Britomart in *The Faerie Queene* through all the forests of Book Three. The central multivalency (history, psychology, religion), the Many-One problem of "Mutabilitie," and the crossing of one "Arthur" with twelve Virtues, all do not depart from allegory's patterned naming of signifier (A) and thing signified (B).

Dante expands the tenor senses into threefold significance, moral, allegorical, anagogical. And he brings the one he started with, the literal vehicle (A) closer to his significance (B) by including it through analogy: Vergil (A) is not only Reason and the Soul-Without-Grace (B)—he is also Vergil in the light of all this: (A) points at all of (B) and is itself enlightened by it.

Still, none of this really helps us in approaching Hamm. Is he, to begin with, (A) or (B), vehicle or tenor? We have no grounds for saying. Call him vehicle, Chess King, or Superego, or Actor. He does not designate them, nor do they enlighten him. In the passionate certainties of Beckett's enigmatic existence, Hamm exemplifies the activities (game, play, feeling, thought, mortal life) that he signifies: such aspects of his being as we have named move repetitiously in the ungrounded conflict of their significance. In Dante's allegorical structure, the real Vergil is enriched by Reason: the real Hamm, while fixedly allegorical in bearing, is impoverished by being seen merely as the Intellect. He struggles against that, and inside it. He is in blind command, as Clov is in limping obedience. Despair? Or else an unblinking look at the fallen condition. What does it mean to be unfallen? Clov and Hamm, Nagg and Nell, are united only in this, that they seem each to have a version of the paradise that has been lost. This may be an illusion, but it is their thought, and their thought is their existence. Still, the play does not present this cogito as a proposition. The play itself is neither Cartesian, nor anti-Cartesian, *pace* Hugh Kenner.

In the structure of this allegory, (A) points to itself, because we cannot initially separate vehicle from tenor. We cannot tell whether we are in a real tower room or in some state for which the tower room stands, and so we do not know whether Hamm is a full person or the abstraction of a person's faculty or activity. He faces his existence uncompromisingly, acts and reacts, wakes up, contemplates as he evades contemplation, never able to come to terms, never ceasing to hope. Dante comes to terms by inventing a *figura* for the rich realities of life: he highlights the realities of this life by reducing them to their ultimate existence in the other life after death. This implies distinctions, the distinction first of all between life and death. Even this distinction cannot be made for *Endgame*. On what ground can it be said that *Endgame* does not in this respect imitate the play that enjoyed great attention in the Paris where Beckett wrote it, *Huis Clos*? Nothing prevents our taking *Endgame* as a purgatorial dialogue of souls after death.

This would make the action a dream, but on what ground can that mode be ruled out for *Endgame*? The blinded Censor Hamm, his white stare terrible as a basilisk's, enthroned in the emptied tower of the mind, tries from his "sleep"-immobilized position, to dominate the mained Libido, which finally decides, after much byplay, perhaps to go out on its own.

"Dreams are licensed as they never were" (Louis Simpson), and dream-interpretation, Freud's or Jung's, analyzes the activities of the unconscious by making, as medieval man did for allegory, a distinction between the story of the dream (A) and its unconscious meaning (B), between manifest and latent content. For Freud a dreamt horse (A) might represent the energy of the libido (B). For Jung the horse would constitute something in its own right, an image out of the collective unconscious, while still representing the libido. Jung would have the horse partake of energy as Dante has Vergil to be partaking of Reason; while Freud is interested in Libido, not horses, as Spenser is interested in chastity at least somewhat more than he is in armed maidens. *Endgame*, though, makes no distinction between manifest content (A) and latent content (B), because we cannot wake from the dream of our existence to analyze it. Taken this way, Beckett appears as more thoroughgoing than the Joyce of *Finnegans Wake*: he uses ordinary language, while Joyce, smelting ordinary language down, necessarily refers to it and so preserves a distinction between the portmanteau words resulting from dream-work and the ordinary words of dream-material. Moreover, the hovering presence of Finnegan's dream prevents Joyce's allegory from being absolutized: the man HCE would not be identified with the city of Dublin in a waking state.

We cannot wake from the dream of our existence; but wanting to analyze it is part of that existence. We dreamed a latent content under the manifest content, we demand the further meanings of allegory; and Beckett gives us *Endgame*. Still, we cannot wake from the dream to analyze it, the analysis is part of the dream. Distortions have taken place, all the mechanisms of the dream-work that Freud analyzes: we are not blind kings or limping servants, our parents are not in the ashcan, we do not inhabit a bare tower on a depopulated plain. The distortion of the manifest content (A) calls for an explanation of a straight meaning (B) which turns out to be (A); there is no straightness, only universal distortion, the world of the Fall, or of the Atom bomb, or of the imperfect pseudo-Cartesian consciousness. Desperate straits, an endgame, evoke desperate maneuvers from the persistent creatures who go on playing while engulfed in desperation.

The aspirations are open, the world has been closed, as the aspiring actors keep saying ("There are no more bicycles." "There are no more coffins." "There is no more pain killer.").

To call this procedure "absurd" is to tip it towards illogicality; it is no more illogical than it is logical. Logic calls for assertions, illogic for contradictions, and here we are given "A is . . . A." The allegory of the play sets up in its auditors a demand for latent content underneath the manifest content, a demand reinforced by its concrete happenings: Clov and Hamm merely insult one another or appeal to one another, and we wish to construct a pattern of latent psychological motive beneath the insults and appeals. Psychological analysis may lay bare the structure of Beckett's kind of dialogue, but only as allegorical analysis might. The enigma of content is left, but the enigma does not dominate the foreground of the action, as it does in Pirandello. The play's framework of allegory forbids our working the Pirandello *cache-cache*: the characters, in being firm allegorical counters, in making gestures that are unconscious, cannot exhibit any quirks or bravura of bepuzzlement.

Beginning with Pirandello and Freud affords Norman N. Holland some brilliant elements of definition:

> Metatheatre, however, leads us into a Promised Land of which Pirandello offers but a dim glimpse: an imitation of nature for an age of psychology. All metatheatre plays (so far as I know) can be explicated as the quite literal and highly realistic playing-out of a psychological (usually psychoanalytic) proposition: Secondary processes of language and number derive from primary processes of sex and aggression (*The Lesson*). Man is a player of eroticized (or cathected) roles (*Balcony*). Language defines its own logic which provides a basis for the displacement and isolation of experience (*Bald Soprano*). Body enslaves mind, each defeating the other, when there is no focus outside the self to do the enslaving (*Godot*).[102]

Leave the *Balcony* aside: Genet fails to achieve Beckett's generality
and power precisely because he does no more than melodramatize
Freud via Pirandello. Holland's admirable summary of *Godot* provides a beginning; and yet Lucky and Pozzo, Vladimir and Estragon,
allegorize more than Body and Mind. The pairs resemble each other
as the enslaved to the enslaved, but also counter each other as the
free (Vladimir and Estragon) to the enslaved, or as the mobile and
changeable (Lucky and Pozzo) to the immobilized and repetitive.
There can be an end only when Godot comes, a little friend known
affectionately by his last name or else the God whose name expands
with a diminutive (*ot*). We can no more know that Godot will not
come than we can know he will come. The last mention of him
leaves this as open as does the first:

VLADIMIR:	We'll hang ourselves tomorrow. (Pause.) *Unless* Godot comes.
ESTRAGON:	And if he comes?
VLADIMIR:	We'll be saved.[103]

If *The Lesson* provides, for its allegorical meaning, just a simple
lesson in the imperfections of sublimation, the title warns us of as
much. And the self-limitations of this one-act fable do not permit
one to reduce *La Cantatrice Chauve* to a fable about the logic of
ordinary language. The Firechief does not speak ordinarily, nor do
the other characters as they stammer off into surrealistic statements
at the end of the play. Trivial chitchat, *Gerede* or *parlerie* in existentialist terms, gathers into its allegorized fits and starts such urgent
ultimates as Death (Bobby Watson), Identity (the guests' discovery
of their marriage), Love (the maid and her poem about the Firechief), Time (the Clock), and Physical Survival or Chance (Guard-
ing against Fires when *tout prend feu*). Thus the trivial is yoked to
the urgent; insisting exclusively on the trivial side of the language
impoverishes the play's actions. They are urgent, as urgent as a fire;
desperate in their very unrelatedness.

Ionesco's tempo, as we might expect, differs from Beckett's; his characters feel and question the urgency, to which those of Ionesco are blind. Hence in Ionesco, the allegorical framework cannot rise, as it does in Beckett, from the gestures of the characters. The allegory is built not by what characters say, but in the deformations of what they say. Beckett's people act allegorically; allegories happen to Ionesco's. The events are *beyond their control*: the dumbness of the orator or the multiplicity of entrances in *Les Chaises*; the filling of the room in *Le Nouveau Locataire*; the increasing metamorphoses in *Rhinocéros*; the growing of the corpse in *Amédée*; the trippling of noses in *Victor*, the intrusion of the mute murderer in *Tueurs sans Gages*. The uncontrollable event, the impulse to start a fire, or the gradual awareness that the city is surrounded by water, or the dominance of erotic rut (A), stands for something that is ineluctably Absurd and unpredictable (B), but is not Absurdity or Unpredictability. Beckett's characters teem with emotion; only to allegorize emotion; they are hyperintelligent: only to schematize intelligence. Ionesco's, though, exhibit a deadness of feeling, a stupidity about what is going on: the deadness and stupidity, too, allegorize something, and the structures of Pirandello remain more visible in his work than in Beckett's, but no more final.

Beckett's allegory is free enough of these structures to allow for greater and greater allegorical condensations: Playing a Tape, Remembering Love, Eating the Unhealthy Banana, put Krapp's solitary and failed existence into heartbreaking rapport with the past he selects from out of the mess at his feet in order that he may hear it, again and again and again. Winnie Gets herself in Deeper and Deeper, and the momentum of her play rises almost hysterically beyond irony, *Happy Days*. The sea is Passion or Life to the declining Ada and Henry of *Embers*, an allegorical Sea because the romantics made it so, and because it is only heard in this radio play. The romantic connotation becomes allegory, the sea (A) becomes the Sea (B is really A). The death of the child under the wheels of her delayed husband's train (A) somehow stands for what the wheezing, childless crone Mrs. Rooney has been bringing to a head the whole day (B) in *All that Fall*. And after the death has been told, there is nothing more to say, only the wind and the rain, and their dragging step, to hear. Literalness is swallowed in unabating sorrow, one allegorical meaning into the other.

Such a human condition as Beckett presents gives Kafka the first term of eschatological complexities whose second term, once more, can never be deduced. Again and again Kafka gives us a pair of signs where the urgency to mediate between them is matched only by the impossibility of mediation. The new arrival and the old villagers (*Das Schloss*), or the castle and the village; those with trials and those without, the accused and the unaccused under the law (*Der Prozess*); the talented and the ordinary (*Josefine*), the audience and the hunger artist, the ape-become-human and men (*Bericht für eine Akademie*), the metamorphosed and the unmetamorphosed (*Die Verwandlung*), the judger and the unwitting judged (*Das Urteil*), the migratory absent and the stationary present (*Der Verschollene: Amerika*), the living and the dead (*Der Jäger Gracchus*), the dog and the musical dogs (*Die Forschung eines Hundes*), horse and man (*der Neue Advocat*), the visitor and the official, the old law and the new (*In der Strafkolonie*) . . . again and again a tale's allegorical abstractions are posed on some such pair.

Moreover, within many tales a given member of the pair may unfold to disclose still other pairs (doctor and patient in *Der Landarzt*; to understand the doctor we must look at further pairs: home and the distant farm, maid and stable boy, earthly horses and unearthly horses). The pattern of generalized allegory stands: Cockroach (A) signifies fallen human condition (B), except that in the story *Die Verwandlung* we also have persons in the human condition (A¹) who act out significations (B¹) which we in turn apply back to the cockroach. We know Gregor Samsa not only by the self-pity he inspires, but by the reactions of terror he inspires in others. A is known by B¹, A¹ by B, and so on. Readings of the cockroach as the sacred scarabaeus of the Egyptians, of Gregor Samsa as a type of Christ

("Waking Samson") enrich connotations, but do not make any beginning at resolving this infinitely extensible structure.

Animals themselves, convenient vehicles for allegory of a reductive sort (Orwell's pigs) or an intensive (Melville's whale), take on a mystery under Kafka's pairings that for a given case may be taken as both reductive (Samsa has lost his human diversity) and intensive (he has come suddenly aware of man's essence)—and yet the significance of the animal does not finally resolve itself either reductively or intensively. Even the simple dog (A) will not stand firmly for attributes of a man (B), and in *Die Forschung eines Hundes* or *Der Bau*, the form of allegory, though set up in the fiction by the circumstance that an animal is said to think, has its translations diverted when animality appears only in an unanimal activity, thought; and when the thought is pitted against another problem (A^1) which would have to find its own signification before the "dog" could be assigned one.

All Kafka's work, completed and uncompleted, hangs fire, like a dream. His stories recount "impossible," dream-like happenings. Moreover, the logical suspensions between the dual terms of his allegories recall Freud's *caveat* in *Die Traumdeutung* that the dream has "no way of representing . . . logical relations" found in ordinary discourse: "if, because, as though, although, either-or."[104] The dream must show these by sequence and other formal shapings of material.

Kafka's formal suspension between one aspect and another in his tales invests their happenings with a sense of dream-like urgency and revelation. The irrational surface gives a powerful impression, as an interpreted dream does for Freud, that its "content is *centered* elsewhere"[105] [Italics Freud's]. So unreal is Doktor Bucephalus, Alexander's horse turned lawyer in *Der Neue Advokat*, that an interpreter cannot dwell on the Swiftian nobility of horses, or on the persistence of legend, or on the absurdity of laws, or on the impenetrability of the old books whose leaves the horse "reads and turns over" in the last sentence of the tale. Allegory poses its own "other meaning": a horse (A) is a lawyer (B); but this is perplexed by a related pair: a legend (A^1) intrudes on the present (B^1); the horse ends by performing an act that brings all four terms into play: by reading old books. Such complexities may turn out to be simple, if man but knew (which by definition he cannot):

> Yes, the whole visible world is perhaps nothing more than the rationalization of a man who wants to find peace for a moment.

> (Ja, die ganze sichtbare Welt ist vielleicht nichts anderes als eine Motivation des einen Augenblick lang ruhenwollenden Menschen.)[106]

The "other" meaning of life may be figured in a trick of vision as in the parable "The Trees":

> For we are like tree trunks in the snow. Apparently they stand smoothly up, and one is supposed to be able to push them away with a slight pressure. No, one cannot do that, for they are bound fast with the ground. But see! even that is only apparent.

> Denn wir sind wie Baumstämme im Schnee. Scheinbar liegen sie glatt auf, und mit kleinem Anstoss sollte man sie wegschieben können. Nein, das kann man nicht, denn sie sind fest mit dem Boden verbunden. Aber sieh, sogar das ist nur scheinbar.[107]

The allegorical likeness is presented through a simile. And the point of likeness recedes from definition, as the operation of vision is contradicted, and contradicted again.

Kafka's allegory acts also through his language, and his firm common style sustains all the simplicity of naming, all the mystery of not being able to name. Josef K says he dies "like a dog," "Wie ein Hund," and the phrase, itself qualified in the final phrase of the novel ("as though he wished the shame to outlive him"), may be either a loose colloquialism, or an allegorical statement that returns us to the wilderness of significance in Kafka's dogs. The simple simile of men as trees in the snow not only evades part of its significance by mentioning snow only once, the way any easy tale would. It opens abruptly on a logical connection, "denn" (for), which is repeated; and there is no way of getting these two occurrences of a logical connective into logical sequence with one another. The adverb of vision, one of Kafka's favorites, is also repeated, an adjective at the same time of logical modality (appearance and reality), "scheinbar." It is the last word in "Die Bäume," and its apparent connections refuse to function either in a loose colloquial way exclusively, or in a tight logical one. The austerity and flatness of the style refers this final word back to the initial interpretation, "scheinbar liegen sie glatt auf." "Scheinbar" remains, first and last, the hidden word of connection; the moral significance of the visual observation disappears into the transparently loose language in which it is clothed. The logical connective "denn," the logical attribution "scheinbar," work as in a dream logic, to distort and not to clarify.

Kafka does not, like Beckett or Ionesco, call language itself into question; he uses it too fluently, too colloquially, for that. His allegory, rather, uses questionableness so masterfully that questions never come incidentally to the surface. His questions reside too essentially in the material, so essentially that Kafka, for all the conventions of his Attic style, alters the novel more radically than Joyce does in *Finnegan's Wake*. Beckett's novels, to the degree that they carry Joyce further, carry him further in the direction of Kafka . . . and surely with Kafka in mind.

Kafka utilized his language in a way new enough to allow Max Bense, without historical disproportion, to base a theory of non-classical signs on the structure of his style *(Die Theorie Kafkas)*:

> . . . the distinction between "sign for something" and "sign of something." A figure, for example, is a sign for a group, a cardinal number. The whistle that I hear may be interpreted as a sign of a nearing train, a sign of something. With a sign of substitutive [*stellvertretenden*] character, a sign *for* some-

thing, the concepts "designata" and "denotata" have an immediately perceptible [*übersehbaren*] significance. With a sign of something, which is always an existential part of that for which it stands,—which it represents just as a sign for something done—the denotating part partially coincides with the designating part. The sign of something can only be iconic, the sign for something can be either iconic or non-iconic.

If a classical theory of signs is to be described with a classical theory of being [*Seinsthematik*], the classical role of the sign appears openly to consist in being a sign for something.

Existential prose is simply the communication of existence, not the communication of the word, the assertion, the intellect.[108]

Kafka's words "denn" and "scheinbar" are like Bense's train-whistles, signs *of* something whose nature they share in as existential parts thereof. They are not signs *for* something, like mathematical figures, to evoke sets and theories of classes. Yet they seem to evoke categories: the class of logical connectives (denn), the class of what is apparent and what is real (scheinbar). They are, as it were, mathematical figures that act like train whistles because they partake of a world wherein men are to be understood with reference to trees-in-the-snow which they themselves perceive, if deceptively (scheinbar).

In his novels, the story is carried along through words whose persistent German abstraction-in-colloquialism asks them to be taken as signs *for* something, like mathematical figures. But the pairings of the allegory, and the colloquialism of the style, root the words existentially in the progress of the narrative, and they function as signs *of* something, moving by like the train whistles of an invisible train, of that inner life before which Kafka wished all to yield: "The sense for the representation of my dreamlike inner life . . . and everything else pushed aside for incidental."

The doubleness of the allegory blurs the designations of the very words that might be taken as clues to work it out. In *Der Prozess*, for example, the first court session is paired with the day of leisure and religion, Sunday. And the courtroom is doubled allegorically by

being set far inside a shabby apartment building. The evasive procedure of the crowded court is doubled by an erotic scene in the
back between a woman and a student. This seems incidental; but the
next week, when that full courtroom is countered by an empty court
room, the woman alone is found in the court, and Josef K's interro-
gation of this woman doubles with their mutual seduction. The
books on the empty bench turn out to be obscene books: the erotic
in the frame of the severe law. Is this true only on that day? The
woman herself can explain all these doublings, possibly; but her
apparently conditional language, itself partaking of this oft-branch-
ing allegorical wilderness, can only produce, not signs for something,
a system that would explain the law; but signs of something, this
particular stage in *Der Prozess*. The language hovers between the
two modes of ultimate abstract definition and incidental colloquial
chatter:

> Es wäre immerhin eine Gefälligkeit, die Sie mir leisten könn-
> ten, wenn Sie dem Untersuchungsrichter oder irgend jeman-
> dem sonst, der wichtige Nachrichten gern verbreitet, mitteil-
> ten, dass ich niemals und durch keine Kunststücke, an denen
> die Herren wohl reich sind, zu einer Bestechung zu bewegen
> sein werde. Es wäre ganz aussichtslos, das können Sie ihnen
> offen sagen. Übrigens wird man es vielleicht selbst schon be-
> merkt haben, und selbst wenn dies nicht sein sollte, liegt mir
> gar nicht so viel daran, dass man es jetzt schon erfährt. Es
> würde ja dadurch den Herren nur Arbeit erspart werden, al-
> lerdings auch mir einige Unannehmlichkeiten, die ich aber
> gern auf mich nehme, wenn ich weiss, dass jede gleichzeitig
> ein Hieb für die anderen ist.[109]

> It would in any case be a favor you could accomplish for me
> if you informed the examining judge, or anyone else at all who
> willingly spreads important news, that never and by none of
> the artifices in which the gentlemen themselves are so rich am
> I to be moved at an act of bribery. It would be wholly with-
> out prospect, that you can tell them openly. Besides, it will
> perhaps already have been noticed, and even if that is not the
> case, it doesn't matter so much to me whether it is known or

> not. It would only, indeed, save the gentlemen some work that
> way; and also, to be sure, for myself, it would save me some
> unpleasantnesses that, however, I willingly take upon myself,
> if I know that each of them is at the same time a blow to
> the others.

Taken just as it runs along colloquially, this speech weaves a maze
of qualifications more worthy of the judge himself than of the clean-
ing woman, who for K cannot really be dissociated from the judges,
her masters *(Herren)*. The language moves its word-counters along
in the Leibnitzian fashion of mere media of exchange, checks for
larger sums drawn on the bank we can never enter.

How modal is the opening subjunctive (wäre) when it is a usual
colloquialism? The same question poses itself for the totality of
"immerhin," the capacity implied in "leisten," the power in "können." Josef K. desperately wants to know what the extent of his
power and his performance may be; but to know that, he would have
to detach this woman enough from her double situation of both
confiding in him and working for the court. She, and her language,
are involved in that double situation, the speech can have meaning
only in it, and yet the meaning of the situation hinges in turn on the
meaning of the speech. The movement from pleasantness ("Gefäl-
ligkeit") to unpleasantnesses ("Unannehmlichkeiten") is accomplished through terms whose abstractness might, in any one case,
be crucial in resolving Josef K's accusation: "Bestechung. . . . aus-
sichtlos. . . . das können Sie ihnen offen sagen."

The woman would undertake unpleasantnesses, through K's favor,
if she could know it would be "a blow for the others at the same
time." Is she deceived, or specially informed, in assuming that anything can be known in this court? Would a blow to the others help
K or only satisfy her? Is her statement an appeal to him, in human
solidarity, or a sexual come-on? Or is it merely the resentment of a
servant against her *Herren?* To solve the allegory, we would have to
resolve the language, but the language points in turn to the doubling
allegory, trying to establish firmly an essentially unstable situation.
The whistling trains glide away on the tracks of the inner life.

So it remains, till K's penultimate encounter with the "religious" (Geistliche) in the darkened cathedral where he has been waiting to conduct a guided tour for business guests. The religious tells him the fable of the doorkeeper, and then offers a Talmudic series of interpretations for the fable. The interpretations double with the fable; the open door of the fable doubles with the fact that the doorkeeper is set to guard it; the fable and interpretation alike double with their setting in *Der Prozess*; and also, as always, with the language of their presentation. "I can speak openly with you," K says, and the religious tells him, incidentally or else finally, not to delude himself, "Täusche dich nicht." In what should I then delude myself? K asks, and the answer provides the cryptic setting for the cryptic story:

> "In dem Gericht täuscht du dich," sagte der Geistliche, "in den einleitenden Schriften zum Gesetz heisst es von dieser Täuschung: vor dem Gesetz steht ein Turhüter."[110]

> "In the court you delude yourself," said the religious. "In the writings introductory to the Law it speaks of this delusion: before the Law stands a doorkeeper."

We might take delusion, "Täuschung," colloquially in passing; or else we might take it as the mode through which the whole fable (and its interpretation too?) must pass. The word comes up again, in the specific interpretations, a "deeper delusion" of the doorkeeper. But, by the end of the interpretations the terms of discussion have changed. "No," said the religious, "all must not be taken for true, it must only be taken for necessary." This statement may define the whole allegory—of the doorkeeper, even of *Der Prozess*. Or else it may simply come along in the colloquial stream. "Sorry meaning," K said, "Lying would be turned into the Order of the World." (Trübselige Meinung . . . Die Lüge wird zur Weltordnung gemacht.) Is K deluded in generalizing lying, or has he broken out of his delusion? The allegory cannot say; and the language cannot move us back to that crucial coordination, of "Täuschung" with "Meinung," because it has moved us ahead. Kafka moves us still farther ahead, to the bodily aspect of the situation in which K remains rooted. This statement, though a concluding one, is not a final judgment, Kafka says, because K was too deep in the strange Kafkan tiredness of body and spirit that in the *Parables* (Paul Goodman and Maurice Blanchot note this especially) makes even Alexander and Poseidon succumb:

> K sagte des abschliessend, aber sein Endurteil war es nicht. Er war zu müde . . .[111]

> K said that in conclusion, but it was not his final judgement. He was too tired . . .

Kafka, like most if not all of the classical allegorists from Dante to Bunyan, orients his meaning towards the spiritual life. This he sees as indeterminate, but he no more despairs of the indeterminacy he schematized than a modern physicist despairs before an indeterminate model of the atom. As Blanchot[112] points out, when Kafka really despairs he becomes dumb. Articulation testifies to freedom, and freedom to hope: writing as prayer. It is of the very uncertainty about his tuberculosis that Kakfa says, "Do I live, then, in the other world? Do I dare to say it?"[113] The article in *"die* andere Welt," makes the other world more certain than any anxiety about his disease. Similarly, in the initial figures of his doubling allegory, the theological realities become displaced, and the meaning of life can only be given by the other life, by death, as Emrich[114] says in concluding his densely woven book of Kafka interpretation. If a general theological sin is figured in the ambiguous special guilt of one man, the reality can be neither arrived at nor departed from: the trial cannot take place or be abrogated. ("Sinfulness is the condition in which we find ourselves, independent of guilt.") The Castle remains separate from the village in the infinite variability of its relation with the village, and K, called directly as no villagers are, remains in infinite variability to them. He is bound to his freedom, in a special way, resembling the others in his subordination to the Castle, differing from them in the mode of his subordination. The most simply called is the most perplexed, the free is least sure of the ground of his freedom. K might be defined by Kierkegaard's ethical categories, but

he remains undefined, and Kafka remains as far from Kierkegaard
in his fable as he does in his language.

> We were made to live in paradise, paradise was set to serve us.
> Our setting had been altered; that this had happened with the
> setting [*Bestimmung*] of paradise, it is not said.[115]

> Theoretically there is given perfect possibility of happiness:
> to believe in the indestructible in oneself and not to strive
> toward it.[116]

> A goal is given, but no way. What we call way is vacillation.[117]

> A belief is like a guillotine, so heavy, so light.[118]

These aphorisms do not remain quite paradoxes: the language avoids
even that. They speak recurrently of paradise, of the other world, of
that towards which Kafka's messianic aspirations tended, as did the
very persistence of his fictions. Their painfulness is rarely a pure
pain, if ever. The allegory doubles too consistently to be fixed singly
on pain. Suffering, he says in another aphorism, does not so much
arise from opposition as mask the fact of opposition (which the tales
never do):

> Only here is suffering suffering. Not as though those who
> suffer here shall be elsewhere exalted because of this suffering
> [*Leiden*], but that what is called suffering in this world, un-
> changed and simply freed from its opposite, is bliss [*Selig-
> keit*].[119]

If suffering here masks bliss in the spiritual world of which this world
is an ambiguous allegory, then the point holds also for the joys of
this world. And Kafka says as much, in the preceding aphorism:

> The joys of this life are not their own, but our anxiety before
> the ascent into a higher life; the torments [*Qualen*] of this
> life are not their own, but our self-torment on account of that
> anxiety.[120]

If one passed the sufferings and bliss of the tales, their joys and
torments and anxiety, through the transforming principles of these
aphorisms, the manifest happenings of *Der Prozess, Die Verwand-*

lung, In der Strafkolonie, Das Schloss would be falsified by their latent happenings: pain would really be bliss, and torment a purification. This is true, but only ultimately. The opposite is true, but only penultimately. The doubleness of the allegory saves them from simplification, even the simplification of paradox. The allegory remains radically perplexing, but it does set forth another meaning, and so does not end in perplexity. The characters may be perplexed, and so may the language they utter, in which their acts are recounted. That is their mode of affirmation.

Kafka gets beyond the "dreadfulness of the barely schematic" *(Das Grauenhafte des bloss Schematischen)*, not by playing humor against contradiction, as Melville did with his "hideous and intolerable allegory," but by relieving the bareness of his schema, by letting it allow freedom, even freedom from itself.

In William Golding's allegories, the religious question about freedom exists within a tight schema, the world of the child, the savage, the dying man. The schema presents a sign *for* necessity: the child is more unconscious than the adult; the savage is less corrupt, and also less intelligent, than the civilized man; the dying man (or the man in purgatory) acts under severely circumscribed conditions. While constituting a sign *for* necessity, the allegorical action poses a sign *of* freedom. The Neanderthal man in *The Inheritors* responds necessarily to a quasi-prelapsarian world where the natural gesture is the right and free one; that world is apprehended through the natural detail presented so vividly in the course of the narrative. Christopher Martin has entered by his first "death" the world of his second death, a free world for its being a world of gradual salvation, though the bare island of purgatorial struggle allows only a dim and gradual realization of the first death. He does not, we do not, perceive that he has died the first death till almost the end of the novel, when it is seen that the boots he kicked off were still on; he cannot die naturally on the island because he has already died naturally in the water. Natural death, recalling one's life and meeting the demand of life on the island, allegorizes the supernatural death, because the latter (B) must in this world be apprehended wholly in terms of the former (A).

Here, in accordance with Bense's notion of a "sign *of* something," the sign partakes of what it signifies: natural death is part of supernatural death, A is part of B. We have no way of knowing, within the novel, how great a part: a part of A may cover all of B (so that A is B, or A is A); the part approaches the whole as its limit. Beckett's equation, A is ... A, stands, so to speak, not as the schema of Golding's allegory, but as a limiting case for it.

The term symbolism would be confusing for such a schema, and also inappropriate. The group of the children on the island in *Lord of the Flies* stands not for some deeper version of itself (as in symbolism), but for the superseding group of men in the world, of which they form a part: a part in two senses—each child is a potential man, children form part of total society. This is a world of necessity, the world of the World whose prince is the Lord of Flies; and its hostilities are brought to a close by a man in uniform who responds to evil not by transcendence but by embarrassment and participative preoccupation. The naval officer, in the final sentence of the novel, is not only trapped in his uniform, engaged in a more inescapable set of hostilities but, in the last free act of the novel, he permits himself —from boredom or else fascination with hostility—to seek out the vessel and figure of war with his eyes:

> ... Ralph wept for the end of innocence, the darkness of man's heart and the fall through the air of the true, wise friend called Piggy.
>
> The officer, surrounded by these noises, was moved and a little embarrassed. He turned away to give them time to pull themselves together; and waited, allowing his eyes to rest on the trim cruiser in the distance.[121]

The children's necessity figures the more inclusive necessity of the adult world. And yet the novel ends in no grand, allegorical act; it

trails off in an allegorical gesture, as small as most of the others in
the texture of the novel. (Golding has said in a lecture that every
smallest detail of his novel is to be taken allegorically.) The world
of freedom cannot enter the schema of the World; it can only enter
the individual consciousness: and at this moment of conclusion the
little child, Ralph, stands closer to the kingdom of heaven than the
proudly rescuing man. Freedom exists only in the awareness of necessity, the weeping for an "end of innocence," "darkness," and "fall."
Freedom partakes of what is essential to innocence, a clear eye and
a loving heart. The shift from part A to whole A, from child to adult,
leaves something over, the unblinking sight of the child, which
makes the part greater than the whole. Similarly, in the shift from
the "dying" Christopher to his rescuers, we are left with the realization that the allegorical significance of his finely rendered grapplings
up and onto the island have been purgatorial in nature, and the shift
of the end involves a transcendence.

The necessity of *The Inheritors* concludes even more cappingly:
the civilized-like false savages (whom H. G. Wells imagines to be
the true ones in the passage Golding cites, with splendid irony, for
his epigraph) have succeeded in supplanting and extinguishing the
"devils," the real prelapsarian Neanderthal man. It is we who are the
inheritors of *both*: most like the corrupt Tuami in the necessity of
our sinfulness, but testifying to what in Christian terms is our capacity for redemption by a greater span of perception and awareness:

> He peered forward past the sail to see what lay at the other
> end of the lake, but it was so long, and there was such a flash-
> ing from the water that he could not see if the line of darkness
> had an ending.[122]

Tuami could see no further, but we can, both technologically and
intellectually, both physically and in the spiritual world which he
allegorizes. The very scheme of the novel constitutes such a transcendence: if our fallen nature predisposes us to act like Tuami, our
very apprehension of Lok's Neanderthal goodness must come from

our desire to make an effort towards the acts he performs with un-fallen effortlessness. Intelligence, if it does not help motive (Tuami is more intelligent than Lok), helps perception (we are more intelli-gent than Tuami), and perception can help motive. Weighted with Tuami, we strive for Lok.

This extrapolates from the novel, but only in the novel's language, which is our own, not Lok's or Tuami's, though in its flexibility it has the freedom to mimic Lok's thought (as he could never mimic ours). The language renders our own natural world with a seemingly unallegorical vividness: this descriptive force strikes Golding's reader perhaps before anything else in his novels. The vividness is unalle-gorical only seemingly: the natural world gives us back the nature of man as well as of the organic life we see about us. Beelzebub is Lord of the *Flies*, and in the novel he (she) is created by one's killing a pig and hanging up the head. Simon, the Christ-like vision-ary, sees the head and swoons before the sight: the rendering hovers into and out of signification, and in this natural world, the transi-tions from one to the other are not discernible:

> Simon looked up, feeling the weight of his wet hair, and gazed at the sky. Up there, for once, were clouds, great bulg-ing towers that sprouted away over the island, grey and cream and copper-colored. The clouds were sitting on the land; they squeezed, produced moment by moment this close, torment-ing heat. Even the butterflies deserted the open space where the obscene thing grinned and dripped. Simon lowered his head, carefully keeping his eyes shut, then sheltered them with his hand. There were no shadows under the trees but every-where a pearly stillness, so that what was real seemed illusive and without definition. The pile of guts was a black blob of flies that buzzed like a saw. After a while these flies found Simon. Gorged, they alighted by his runnels of sweat and drank. They tickled under his nostrils and played leap-frog on his thighs. They were black and iridescent green and with-out number; and in front of Simon, the Lord of the Flies hung on his stick and grinned. At last Simon gave up and looked back.[123]

Simon's allegorical gestures of looking up, lowering his head, covering his eyes, giving up and looking back, respond to physical sensations that, through the response, themselves partake of the allegory. The butterflies are "real" and signs *of* loveliness: but not symbols *for* it. The natural world moves by like Kafka's moral world, like Bense's train whistles—though these train whistles are not invisible but visible. The real is illusive, "because of a pearly stillness," qualified by the indefinite article, "*a* pearly stillness, so that what was real seemed illusive and without definition." The allegory offers a schema of definition that rises from, and does not fit, the totality of the natural world.

At every point in *Pincher Martin* a natural appearance (A) is immersed in the supernatural reality (B) which in this life it cannot, by definition, reach (A remains A). In *The Inheritors* Lok's stream of consciousness, not distinguishing between a sight and an idea ("picture"), carries the natural world along in its flow of perception, a perception that, in the allegory of the novel, is moral without Lok's unfallen self needing to draw the moral in any way:

> The trees on the island acquired definition, the birch trunk
> that overtopped them was suddenly silver and white. Across
> the water on the other side of the gap the cliff still harbored
> the darkness but everywhere else the mountains exhibited
> their high snow and ice.[124]

The verbs, "acquired definition," "harbored," "exhibited," set out the relation of the natural world to a consciousness that, in lacking selfconsciousness, becomes a consciousness of *it*.

Sammy Mountjoy in *Free Fall* perceives similarly, because he cannot grasp his consciousness of freedom; it vanishes in "the taste of potatoes." "I could take whichever I would of these paths. There was nothing to draw me down one more than the other. I danced down one for joy in the taste of potatoes. I was free, I had chosen." This is the experience, whose "definition" had come earlier: "Free-will cannot be debated but only experienced, like a color or the taste of potatoes." A painter is speaking, whose moral perceptions work through the senses he will, in turn, question again for definition; and will experience beyond the definition.

Sammy's exemplary nature verges on allegory through the typicality of his experience: Childhood in a Slum, Religion versus Science, Love, Revolutionary Thought, War. The part-whole schema appears here not in setting Mountjoy against some other (child against adult, resurrected man against dying man, innocent savage against corrupt savage) but in his being set against the wholeness of an experience he can only partially account for. The title suggests both physics (free fall as the drop of a physical object unimpeded) and metaphysical theology (free fall as Adam's situation, "sufficient to have stood though free to fall"). So, too, the duality in the world of experience, necessity (science) and freedom (for Golding, the archetype) are felt as coexisting through perception just because they do not get together. The physical detail does not fall in with an allegorical schema: it opens the possibility of allegory, freely:

> Agincourt was a great victory; but Jacob laid his head on a stone—I saw how hard it was and uncomfortable—and dreamed of a ladder of gold that reached into heaven. Watt invented the steam-engine; but a voice spoke to Moses out of a bush that burned and was not consumed away.[125]

The world of necessity, here, is represented by a freely loving man (Nick Shale) in whose scientific law the burning bush must be consumed; the world of Biblical freedom is represented by a woman bound in hostilities. "I hung for an instant between two pictures of the universe; then the ripple passed over the burning bush and I ran towards my friend." Definition, he goes on to say, closes a door he was not to knock on again until the prison camp, where freedom becomes a seduction to betray the self, a seduction by a doctor who "does not know about peoples," in the broken words of the novel's concluding phrase.

Who does? Not Sammy; he cannot know a person, and cannot stand for knowing a person's freedom. He can only be free, wondering about how he was determined. The greatest sense of freedom comes under the greatest dominance of necessity, in the prison camp; where the natural world, for the painter, has become charged with perceptions, of total moral connection, and the more intensely physical for that. The physical world (A) seems to bear its allegorical signatures (B); the novel has the stiffness of the exemplary about it. Sammy, a "real" unallegorical person set in allegorical situations, rises to the signs in his perceptions, signs *of* freedom as convincing as though they were signs *for* freedom:

> I walked between the huts, a man resurrected but not by him. I saw the huts as one who had little to do with them, was indifferent to them and the temporal succession of days that they implied. So they shone with the innocent light of their own created nature. I understood them perfectly, boxes of thin wood as they were, and now transparent, letting be seen inside their quotas òf sceptred kings. I lifted my arms, saw them too, and was overwhelmed by their unendurable richness as possessions, either arm ten thousand fortunes poured out for me. Huge tears were dropping from my face into dust; and this dust was a universe of brilliant and fantastic crystals, that miracles instantly supported in their being.[126]

Perception is a miracle, like freedom, the perception of a man free, who has been freed. His fellow prisoners are "sceptered kings," a metaphor that is allegorical, and visual, because it comes from the child's throw-away cigarette-box cards of the "Kings of Egypt"; the real situation of living in a city at the novel's time of writing is mined with the allegorical survivals. The novel has begun with the kings:

> I have walked by stalls in the market-place where books, dog-eared and faded from their purple, have burst with a white hosanna. I have seen people crowned with a double crown, holding in either hand the crook and the flail.[127]

There is no end to the kings: they may enter Sammy's perceptions freely, in a wholly new role: men in prison camp. And always allegorically: that is how they began. The purple is literal, and also allegorical: it has been put in the book first of all, remotely but unmistakably, because of the royal association. In Sammy's perception, at least, and that is all that here is set to count. The "white hosanna" bursts the visual world over into an apocalyptic one, whose synesthetic significance sets allegory out in a great leap, from the beginning. We plot the leap itself. That is the freedom, of which the allegory is a sign, yet for which its schemata cannot be adequate. This Pilgrim can never progress, because progress is total. Or he is already *there*.

: V :

ACTION

THE LANGUAGE of a classical play relates to the action of the play by reciting about it. The recitation may be about what is present before our eyes on the stage, an expository recitation of what confronts us directly, as at the beginning of *Oedipus Rex*, when we are given a summary of the plague that has brought the suppliants to the king's feet. Or it may be about the past, the birth of Dionysus in the *Bacchae*. The playwright of "bourgeois realism" presents such information indirectly, as in the seemingly digressive gossip of servants when the curtain goes up. The recitativeness of classical drama, again, has language take over for violent action, in the convention that strong physical action be recounted by a messenger instead of being shown on stage. But Uncle Vanya attempts murder and Stanley Kowalski begins rape before our very eyes.

This recitativeness pervades the classical theatre. In the *Agamemnon* of Aeschylus, when Clytemnestra speaks after the offstage murder and uses three demonstrative words (*houtos, tesde, tade*), she is not demonstrating information we do not possess: we know the corpse is Agamemnon, we know she killed him:

> This is Agamemnon, my
> Husband, a body dead by this right hand,
> The deed of a just doer. These facts are thus.

A modern play, whether or not it showed the murder on stage, would not have a character put it this way. Clytemnestra's pride and self-justification in this speech, her queenly imperiousness as she lays

128

down to the chorus how matters stand ("these facts are thus"), would be rendered "indirectly" by gesture. Her bold pride might be revealed with an order: "Take away this body." Her self-justification could be shown by an intimate conversation with Aegisthus in which she adduced some parallel case. Her imperiousness might emerge from some act or command to the chorus in which, by implication and not by statement as here, she assumed that the existence of these facts thus (*tad'hod'echei*) would not alter the status quo.

Oedipus, too, recites his ideas and feelings, from his ritual assertion of help for the state, right through to his broken self-banishment and prediction about his daughters' unhappiness. In a modern play he would not speak so ominously of the daughters in their presence. In *Oedipus Rex*, though, he does not predict their unhappiness in order to act upon them: he merely recites it, and so it does not matter that they are there. They are defined as "mute persons," those who by definition do not recite. Only three reciters, stiff and fixed in their boots and masks, are allowed on the Greek stage at a time. When they become silent, the mobile chorus chants a further recitation about the action.

The characters of Racine, too, do not act so much as reveal by recitation the intensity of feelings that have already been formed. They try to act and cannot: hence the tragedy. Pyrrhus, in putting pressure on Andromaque, only recites his passion; she does not capitulate on stage but only counters by a recitation of her devotion to a husband's memory. Oreste is already prepared to do anything for Hermione, and her request that he murder Pyrrhus is not "meant," but only a recitation of Hermione's conflict between pride and frustrated love. She does not "persuade" him to obey her, because obedience is already implicit in his devotion; as her own rejection of the murder is already implicit in her deep-felt dutifulness at the outset. The passions do not change through the action: they unfold through being pressed to the revelation of recitation.

M. C. Bradbrook's vivid reconstruction of delivery in the Jacobean

theatre gives some idea of the context in which recitation was the
natural mode of dramatic utterance:

> In a repertory company, which played with spectators on
> the stage and in broad daylight, it would be very difficult to
> sink the actor in his part, especially if he were alone on the
> forestage and soliloquising. The audience's eyes would not be
> concentrated automatically as they are in a darkened theatre,
> and hearing would be more difficult in the open air. To main-
> tain attention it would be necessary to exaggerate movement
> or statuesqueness, to use inflated delivery and conventional
> posture . . . At all events, the acting was probably nearer to
> that of the modern political platform or revivalist pulpit than
> that of the modern stage.[128]

On this panoramic Elizabethan-Jacobean stage, the recitative convention holds through all the fluidity of action and extravagance
or inwardness of statement. Consider the scene in Heywood's *A
Woman Killed with Kindness*, where the steps of seduction between Wendoll and Mistress Frankford are recited, not rendered by
nuance but bluntly declared. Just before this, in a series of asides,
Wendoll has recited every step of his own vacillation before the
ingratitude and sin of making a declaration to the wife of his kind
employer. She begins in ignorance, and he recites his love with the
bare statement of it:

ANNE: Are you not well, sir, that ye seem thus troubled?
    There is sedition in your countenance.

WENDOLL: And in my heart, fair angel, chaste and wise.
    I love you! Start not, speak not, answer not.
    I love you—nay, let me speak the rest.
    Bid me to swear, and I will call to record
    The host of heaven.

ANNE: The host of heaven forbid
    Wendoll should hatch such a disloyal thought![129]

She does not so much try to work on him as recite the ideas that ought to work on him. "Is it to me you speak?" she says, not as an evocation of respect, but as a recitation of what her position is. When he answers, still once more, with an expanded recitation of his love, she responds not by gesture or declaration but by a recitation of her response:

WENDOLL: . . . For you I'll love, and in your love I'll die.

ANNE: You move me, sir, to passion and to pity.
The love I bear my husband is as precious
As my soul's health.[130]

His recitation of an equal love for her husband, of an intent for secrecy, moves her to an only momentary loss of words:

ANNE: What shall I say?
My soul is wand'ring, and hath lost her way.
O, Master Wendoll! Oh!

WENDOLL: Sigh not, sweet saint,
For every sigh you breathe draws from my heart
A drop of blood.

ANNE: I ne'er offended yet.
My fault, I fear, will in my brow be writ.
Women that fall, not quite bereft of grace,
Have their offenses noted in their face.
I blush and am ashamed. O Master Wendoll,
Pray God I be not born to curse your tongue
That hath enchanted me! This maze I am in
I fear will prove the labyrinth of sin.[131]

If this were not in a recitative tradition, we might call the representation here wooden and unmotivated. But Heywood, while a minor playwright, is not a naive one, and the psychology presented in this scene is both gradual and complex. The sense of sin in succumbing to it, the pretended appeal to virtue as a real appeal to sin, the feminine appeal to the devoted sinner for support in a virtue that is really a commencement of sin ("O, Master Wendoll! Oh!"), the struggle of chastity as itself an inducement to erotic pleasure-pain

("Sigh not, sweet saint")—all these complex motions, gradually arrived at, unfold a psychological action that is anything but pat, exaggerated or contrived. These gestures, however, are present not in action but in a series of reciting statements that do set them out patly on the stage. Where Chekov or Ibsen would hint and suggest, Heywood merely states.

The language recites the action in Shakespeare too, initially, though his great emotional resonance does take him outside these categories. Othello's final speech, or Fortinbras', put into language what our stage would convey by hint or gesture. Coriolanus need only recite the words, "There is a world elsewhere," and we understand that an epochal decision has transformed this character. Here the recitation is far more pat even than in Heywood's declaration. The opening of *King Lear*, which bothers so many critics, comes clearer in the light of the recitative convention. It may be taken as a sort of theatrical condensation of processes which "actually" would take place over a long time. King Lear would not "really" ask Goneril, Regan, and Cordelia for declarations of love, and then verbally bestow pieces of a kingdom on the first two, any more than Mistress Frankford would "really" tell Wendoll her thoughts before she was quite ready to give in. Lear does not act out a realistic appeal for filial devotion, and his scene is ridiculous only in the light of modern dramatic conventions. No pre-Christian Britain sophisticated enough to contain an Edgar and a Goneril would be primitive enough for such a scene really to take place. Lear recites the appeal for filial devotion, as Clytemnestra recites, rather than exhibits, the pride and self-justification of the murderess. Or take this speech from the recognition scene in *Pericles*, which should probably be spoken as that recitation to the audience, the aside, though such a stage direction is not appended to it:

PERICLES: I am great with woe, and shall deliver weeping.
            My dearest wife was like this maid, and such a one
            My daughter might have been. My queen's square brows;
            Her stature to an inch: as wand-like straight;

As silver voic'd; her eyes as jewel-like
And cas'd as richly: in pace another Juno;
Who starves the ears she feeds, and makes them hungry
The more she gives them speech. Where do you live?[132]

If Pericles is interrogating Marina, he "ought not" to recite his
thoughts in her presence, especially when he is as politic a person
as we have already seen him to be. He has been grieved to muteness;
now, moved to speak, he begins by reciting his grief. The speech
does not render or delineate motive but merely recites it, however
complex it may be. "I will believe thee," he shortly says; but goes on
interrogating her. The stages of recognition get recited one by one,
so little inwardly that we cannot isolate any one speech as recording
the moment of Pericles' conviction. No speech breaks out with conviction, because all the speeches recite conviction as it is growing.

To think out loud, to soliloquize, is to recite motive before or
after taking action on it. Hamlet recites why he will not kill the
praying king, and the king rises from prayer to recite why he believes
the prayer to have been ineffective.

When language *recites* about action, language stands to action as
one manifest content to another manifest content. (The borrowed
terms, again, are those of Freudian dream analysis.) Everything happens on the surface, word or deed. Much may happen of great sub-
tlety—Shakespeare is peerless. But it happens through a gorgeous
surface of language: through poetry. Even a play composed entirely
of prose, Jonson's *Epicene*, may recite its action: language here, too,
manifests itself, *as* prose (against a poetic convention).

In our tradition of bourgeois realism (if we may continue to use
this ambigious and oversimplifying term), from Ibsen to Pirandello,
the language *uncovers* the action. Motive is rendered, not recited,
and the language stands to the action as manifest to latent insofar
as the language reveals attitudes of which the speaker is unaware:
old Werle is somewhat unaware that he is being hostile to Hjalmar
Ekdal when he calls him "thirteenth at table." He does not say "I

rather despise you, and you don't belong here": he does not recite his attitude. He uncovers it, and behind the manifest language lies the latent attitude.

So little Hedvig does not say, "I will kill myself," as Othello says, "And smote him thus." She depreciates herself, sinks in the feeling of being unwanted; and this manifest language turns out to be a latent expression of a motive that does become manifest, and silent when she commits suicide. The scene of something latent underlying something manifest is present not only in the title of the play "The Wild Duck." We may see the language uncovering action from the very outset, and beneath everything manifest lies something latent.

This relation between manifest and latent holds for the setting too. While the stage of the classical or the Jacobean play is relatively bare, the stage of Ibsen is fully laid out, and its represented space has latent psychological implications as well as manifest physical ones. *The Wild Duck* opens on a "handsome and comfortably furnished study." At the back are folding doors which have been thrown open and the portierès drawn back—Werle has let his guests psychologically as well as physically into the intimacy of his house. In the front, "the lamps are lit and have green shades, producing a soft light in the room,"—and we have been given, as the curtain goes up, a latent physical correlative for the physical defect on which the play turns, Werle's weakening sight, and the oncoming blindness, known only to him, of his illegitimate daughter Hedvig. Sight-blindness itself may be taken to symbolize the whole labyrinth of honesty-deception which is the play's central theme: Werle wants light, but not too much, because he has weak eyes; because he has a clear head he wants light, but because he has weak morals he wants not too much. The illusion of comfort and honesty that Mrs. Sörby provides, finds its visual counterpart here in "a soft light." Upstage there is even more light, ". . . a room, brightly lit with lamps and branch candlesticks." The latent connection between Werle's personal comfort and his "secret" business practises also receives a manifest physical representation on the space of the stage, "A small, private door, on the right hand side of the study, leads to the office." Pettersen's gesture, and his statement, to Jensen, in the play's opening words, are latent with significances of which he is not aware:

PETTERSEN: (lighting a lamp on the mantelpiece and putting a shade over it) Hark at 'em, Jensen; the old man's up now, making a long speech to propose Mrs. Sörby's health.

JENSEN: (moving a chair forward) Do you think what people say about those two is true, that there's something between them?

PETTERSEN: Goodness knows.

JENSEN: He's been a gay old dog in his time, hasn't he?

PETTERSEN: Maybe.[133]

Pettersen knows more than Jensen; we will know more than either, but as yet we cannot know how much. Pettersen will not tell all he knows; he will *not* recite, unlike the guards on Hamlet's battlement. Under this "ordinary conversation" a half-understood hedonism is suggested ("gay old dog"), and beyond that the suggestion of secrets which might qualify or negate an apparent hedonism ("Maybe"). The moment that Pettersen's statement arrests in the play's first words does not recite; it merely points out, in the fascinated-disgusted attention of the pausing servant, the gesture by which Werle symbolically commands and participates in a toast to Mrs. Sörby's health (when he and his illegitimate daughter are sick in the eyes). He and his housekeeper will turn out to welcome marriage because, as this described gesture of merely public cheer implies, they are willing to forget much, to manage each other and know, each, that he is being managed. A less brazen businessman would not toast his mistress-housekeeper when he intended to marry her, until he had married her. A less sophisticated one would not simultaneously flaunt her and be willing to marry her. Let Gregers protest, let Gina have been shunted off, let Hedvig die—none of it can make the slightest difference to the collusive festivity of this pair. Werle and Mrs. Sörby are utterly without rancor. They have kindness, but no heart. Under the manifest content of Pettersen's words all this latent content has begun to appear.

The masterly economy of Ibsen's dramatic construction differs from that of a well-made French play precisely in enlisting and coordinating such latent content.

The characters are able to act on each other because the latent content of what they say constitutes a pressure which even they cannot fully control. In what is perhaps the key interchange in the play, Hedvig hears Gregers' latent implication, as he himself (his father's son) proceeds, boldly unaware of the latent possibilities (hostility, etc.) in what he is saying:

GREGERS: (coming nearer to her). But now, suppose you sacrificed the wild duck, of your own free will, for his sake?

HEDVIG: (getting up) The wild duck?

GREGERS: Suppose now you gave up for him, as a free-will offering, the dearest possession you have in the world?

HEDVIG: Do you think it would help?

GREGERS: Try it, Hedvig.

HEDVIG: (gently, with glistening eyes). Yes, I will try it.

GREGERS: Have you really the strength of mind to do it, do you think?

HEDVIG: I will ask grandfather to shoot the wild duck for me.

GREGERS: Yes, do. But not a word about anything of the kind to your mother.

HEDVIG: Why not?

GREGERS: She doesn't understand us.[134]

The *double-entendres* of dramatic irony in this interchange depend on a complexity of latent effects uncovered by the speeches: manifestly friendly, Gregers is not honest enough to curb his latent hostility. Being self-centered, he cannot see Hedvig for other than rational, as she manifestly seems here.

In *Ghosts*, Oswald's free-association into manifest poetry signalizes to his mother that he is going insane:

OSWALD: Because it doesn't necessarily have a fatal end quickly, the doctor said. He called it a kind of softening of the brain—or something of that sort. (Smiles mournfully). I think that expression sounds so nice. It always made me think of cherry-coloured velvet curtains—something that is soft to stroke.[135]

MRS. ALVING: (With a scream) Oswald!

Her scream calls him back from the borderland of manifest "idiotic" delectation into the latency of thinking the erotic thoughts that his hereditary syphilis forbids him:

OSWALD: (jumps up and walks about the room). And now you would have taken Regina from me! If I had only had her. She would have given me a helping hand, I know.

The depths that the "cherry-coloured velvet curtains" threaten to surface, give way to the interaction of latencies. To this interaction the potent visual-poetic effect of "cherry-coloured velvet" does not stand as a recitative and decorative center, the way such detail might in Shakespeare. "A rich jewel in an Ethiop's ear," does stand for Juliet; at the dance it heightens her white skin in the night.*

The mention of cherry-coloured velvet curtains, however, uncovers what had been latent, the limit across which, through which, Oswald is to lapse, while for the moment his mother's scream, and her force of will, prevent him.

---

*Distantly, it may suggest the drugged girl on her bier when she seems to be taken by the dark angel of death. In the light of King Hamlet's death ("into the porches of his ear did pour") it does not seem completely fanciful to read the *ear* is a suggestion of the Capulet vault.

Here the latent content in action underlying the language already verges on a delineation of something like the Freudian unconscious, as *Peer Gynt* in its own way also does.

Chekov, who puts his plays together differently, also employs language to uncover action. Take the end of *The Sea Gull*:

SHAMRAEV:	(leads Trigorin to the cupboard) Here's the thing I was speaking about just now (takes the stuffed sea-gull from the cupboard). This is what you ordered.
TRIGORIN:	(looking at the sea-gull). I don't remember it. (Musing) I don't remember. (The sound of a shot coming from right of stage; everyone starts).
MADAME ARKADIN:	(frightened). What's that?
DORN:	That's nothing. It must be something in my medicine-chest that has gone off. Don't be anxious (goes out door on right, comes back in half a minute). That's what it is. A bottle of ether has exploded. (Hums) "I stand before thee enchanted again . . ."
MADAME ARKADIN:	(sitting down to the table). Ough, how frightened I was. It reminded me of how . . . (Hides her face in her hands) It made me quite dizzy . . .
DORN:	(turning over the leaves of the magazine, to Trigorin) There was an article in this two months ago—a letter from America— and I wanted to ask you, among other things (puts an arm round Trigorin's waist and leads him to the footlights) as I am very much interested in the question . . . (In a lower tone, dropping his voice) Get Irina Nikolayevna away somehow. The fact is, Konstantin Gavrilovitch has shot himself. . .[136]

The language manifests so little, and uncovers the latent disposi-
tions of the ruminating characters so much, that Dorn is able to
carry off the famous double-take, of suicide—exploded bottle—suicide, by merely training his casual conversation along the digressive
current. The tune he hums (with its latent significance for the lovers
in the play) is in words, but otherwise it scarcely differs from his
"indifferent" gestures, turning the leaves of a magazine, putting his
arm round Trigorin's waist. Trigorin, to the end, is egotistically dis-
tracted: he does not call himself so, but his words "I don't remember" uncover the distraction. Madame Arkadin's language reveals
the self-centeredness of the prima donna in the very way it com-
municates the disturbance over her son's possible suicide. Dorn need
not, perhaps, feign so much; they are paying little attention to him.
He has to drag Trigorin away, and he humors him so that he will
"get Irina Nikolayevna away somehow." These characters do not
answer the manifest statement of another's speeches; they pick up
the latent drift, and produce, through their own disjunctions of
manifest statement, another current of latent drift. The play is an
emotional music—much is said, but more is left unsaid. No one
speech uncovers the action, but all the speeches together reveal a
music of action they are uncovering while the latent cry is heard in
their manifest designations:

VARYA: (through her tears). Mamma, that's not a joking
           matter.
LOPAHIN: "Ophelia, get thee to a nunnery."
GAEV: My hands are trembling; it's a long while since I
           had a game of billiards.
LOPAHIN: "Ophelia! Nymph, in thy orisons be all my sins
           remembered."
LYUBOV: Come, it will soon be supper-time.
VARYA: How he frightened me! My heart's simply throb-
           bing.
LOPAHIN: Let me remind you, ladies and gentlemen: on the
           22nd of August the cherry orchard will be sold.
           Think about that! Think about it![137]

Pirandello launches an endless chain of speculation within a play because his language never lets a manifest statement stand. Consequently, what the latent meaning of a given statement may be is always ambiguous in itself, and examining it by further statements (themselves ambiguous) increases the ambiguity both ways. This process is endless, because the words the characters use to come to terms with earlier words and acts this way, just keep intensifying their susceptibility to ambiguous interpretative words and responding intuitive actions. Without the manifest-latent conventions of Ibsen and Chekov, Pirandello would lack the first term and the necessary representational framework for his procedures.*

And Brecht's *Verfremdungseffekt* in actual practice, does not so much alienate and objectify the actor's feeling—how could it?—as restore a purified recitative to the stage; of this his songs are also fine examples.

In modern allegorical plays of the "absurd" kind, there is given no realistic point of reference by which we can tell whether any given speech or act is latent or manifest initially. The rope which Pozzo has around Lucky's neck in *Waiting for Godot* may be taken mani-

*However, the convention of language in bourgeois realism, which makes for the success of Pirandello, almost always makes for the failure of the modern verse play. The manifest language of poetry points to its own artifice and tries to recite, which works in the recitative convention but in the "realistic" convention is well-nigh fatal. When language must uncover action, it cannot call attention to itself at the same time: it cannot both uncover and recite in a realistic setting. Eliot, in desperation, has buttressed his lame plays with an indefensible theory that poetic dialogue should efface itself, not call attention to itself. Shakespeare's verse in dialogue may not be as richly tapestried as Milton's or Mallarmé's, but it does call attention to itself, while Ibsen's language effaces itself, as Eliot claims dramatic verse should. Eliot's only play that rings fully true is *Murder in the Cathedral*, which is not built as a realistic play but exists somewhere between the medieval Morality and the Brechtian historical exemplum. If he had finished *Sweeney Agonistes*, we might have had a new vein for the verse play, the near-musical comedy, a companion piece for *Les Mamelles de Tirésias* and the *Dreigroschenoper*.

Claudel succeeds by harking back to the earlier convention. Giving his characters an open panoramic stage, investing them with tremendous passions, he is able to put manifest, Elizabethan-like language in their mouths without allegorizing them away from an imaginably realistic but exotic situation.

festly as a real one and latently as an allegorical one (standing for oppression, or authority, or circumscription, or "a generalized act"). Consequently, all that Pozzo says, all that is said about him, simultaneously recites what is manifest and uncovers what is latent. Language relates to action in "absurd" plays not just as manifest to manifest, the recitative case, and not just as manifest to latent, the Ibsenian one. Beckett's language manifestly enters the sphere of action, and it also latently creates the action. In its particular poetic intensity (Beckett) or intellectual vivacity (Ionesco), the language circles the action, extends it, and also undermines it. Taken as manifest speech around an action that never emerges from latency, it is close to phatic communication, *Gerede* or *parlerie*, a mere murmuring before the void: "nothing happens." Taken as latent speech striking the deepest chords in the play, as *Rede*, it both expresses and motivates a total action with a generality of allegorical application: "everything happens." No realistic plot exists in such a play to serve for the point of reference that would simplify this structure. In *Endgame* either Hamm is coming to terms momentously with death and Clov working up to the momentous decision to leave for good: "everything happens"; or else all these gestures of speech circle the same old round, "nothing happens." But what they say is either, and so both.

Hence all the speeches sound like condensed and dissolved soliloquies: they sum up a situation as a laconic Hamlet might; they fail somehow to reach the auditor, as the nostalgic speakers of Chekov are never quite heard. At the same time the speeches trigger interaction, much as Gregers Werle does when he works latently on Hedvig. The dissolved soliloquies of these speeches allow for the hidden evolution of motive. There is dramatic interaction between the speeches, and at the same time a lack of interaction, on the "simplest" level; as we may see by pausing over a passage:

ESTRAGON: Ah stop blathering and help me off with this bloody thing.

VLADIMIR:	Hand in hand from the top of the Eiffel Tower, among the first. We were respectable in those days. Now it's too late. They wouldn't even let us up. (Estragon tears at his boot.) What are you doing?
ESTRAGON:	Taking off my boot. Did that never happen to you?
VLADIMIR:	Boots must be taken off every day, I'm tired telling you that. Why don't you listen to me?
ESTRAGON:	(feebly). Help me!
VLADIMIR:	It hurts?
ESTRAGON:	(angrily). Hurts! He wants to know if it hurts!
VLADIMIR:	(angrily). No one ever suffers but you. I don't count. I'd like to hear what you'd say if you had what I have.
ESTRAGON:	It hurts?
VLADIMIR:	(angrily). Hurts! He wants to know if it hurts!
ESTRAGON:	(pointing). You might button it all the same.
VLADIMIR:	(stopping). True. (He buttons his fly.) Never neglect the little things of life.
ESTRAGON:	What do you expect, you always wait till the last moment.
VLADIMIR:	(musingly). The last moment ... (He meditates.) Hope deferred maketh the something sick, who said that?
ESTRAGON:	Why don't you help me?
VLADIMIR:	Sometimes I feel it coming all the same. Then I go all queer. (He takes off his hat, peers inside it, feels about inside it, shakes it, puts it on again.) How shall I say? Relieved and at the same time ... (he searches for the word) ... appalled. (With emphasis) AP-PALLED. (He takes off his hat again, peers inside it) Funny. (He knocks on the crown as though to dislodge a foreign body, peers into it again, puts it on again.) Nothing to be done.[138]

The characters both speak to themselves and speak to each other. They both move ahead, moved by response to the speech of the other (and to the preoccupations with the self). They move emotionally, exhibiting primal gestures of unconscious action, as when Estragon goes weak under intellectual attack ["(feebly), 'Help me!' "]. Then, at frustration, he goes angry, triggering Vladimir's anger; to which, in turn, he responds, freed of anger, with a question ("It hurts?"). The persistence of Vladimir's anger gives Estragon the upper hand, allows him to criticize Vladimir for a neglect that has sexual overtones, leaving his fly open. This motion gets nowhere ("Nothing to be done"). And yet every speech activates a response. The play consists of a big series of motions always ready to make the big leap forward, never making it. Perhaps the very dialogue is preventing them from making it. . . . In the interaction here, characteristically, Estragon is obsessed with appealing for help; Vladimir is obsessed with philosophically ignoring the appeal. Each for himself is obsessed with something manifestly physical and latently allegorical, Estragon with his boots, Vladimir with his hat.

Charged as they are with both latent and manifest content, each single one of these speeches constitutes an intense answer and reaction to the speech before. The theatricality of dramatic interplay is as though coiled into the gaps between the speeches. It is this dramatic effectiveness that permits the speeches to be taken for condensations—for allegorizations—of longer speeches. Estragon's first speech, "help me off with this bloody thing," in the indeterminate allegory of Beckett's stage, can be taken as signifying an intellectual appeal, complete with emotional accompaniment, to any kind of salvage or rescue action, to any enlistment of assistance in the practical sphere: it could stand for Henry IV talking at great length to Gloucester as well as for Falstaff talking to Bardolph.

Vladimir's answer reacts by denying the practical sphere: he dreams of a past excursion to the Eiffel Tower. And the Chekovian drift is intensified, through the allegorical frame, not only to an opposition between practical sorry present and contemplative glorious past: the present reacts to the past, condenses and transforms the past. Everything charges the language with happening *just because* nothing happens. Many plays are less theatrical because they opt for allegory. Allegory, through Beckett's intensive speeches, makes his dialogue more theatrical. Estragon's reactive answer, again, tries to recall Vladimir from the Eiffel tower dream back to reality, and to a personal appeal. Vladimir responds this time, fully, colloquially and allegorically all at once. And with magnificent condensation. One could imagine a play, opposing Estragon the bungling man of action to Vladimir the ineffective poet, which would present in the space of four acts no more than the interaction implied by these few speeches.

This language contains latent emotion: it evokes a response. It is manifestly intellectual: it sums up philosophically, again and again. Its manifest emotion may also be latent: emotional interaction may be ultimately "all there is." The manifest intellections may themselves reveal something latent: emotional attitudes (Vladimir pretends to think but is actually withdrawing from human contact) or else a metaphysical situation (to have intellectual attitudes is the best way to "wait for Godot"; and to wait, perhaps the best way to manifest hope: "Faith is the substance of things hoped for, the evidence of things unseen").

Similarly in *Endgame*, when Nagg, the whitefaced father in an ashcan, calls for his sugar-plum; Hamm, the redfaced blind son in a wheel chair, answers him by sneering his way through the Lord's Prayer. Hamm is answering his father, thereby interacting with him. And the father is also answering the son: the father's manifest appeal may be a form, ultimately, of latent sneer to the son whom he let cry when he was a baby. Hamm's sneer, ultimately, may be an appeal to the father who still won't listen. But Nagg can love too: his sugar-plum narcissism leads to altruism towards Nell, while Hamm can no longer love. Hamm's sneer would then be a stronger form of appeal: it reveals a stronger latent need, or a stronger awareness of need. The latent and the manifest of this language circles

action, becomes action, rises out of action, falls back into the total
ground of action. Every move counts in the *Endgame*, every word.
Counts doubly: the game hangs on every move. Counts not at all:
the game is already won or lost, the powers of the players utterly
given.

Ionesco, who constructs his action differently, gets correspond-
ingly full effects, latent and manifest, from his language and action.
In *Les Chaises*, all the statements either manifest what the stage
will not because the chairs and the guests must be imagined on
stage, not appearing physically when spoken of. Or else the statements uncover the latent fantasy of the couple: we see with our own
eyes that they refer to nonexistent chairs and guests:

> LA VIEILLE, à la Dame: —Une vie modeste mais bien remplie
> . . . Deux heures par jour, il travaille à son message.
> On entend sonner. Depuis très peu d'instants, on
> entendait le glissement d'une embarcation.
>
> LA VIEILLE, au Vieux: —Quelqu'un. Va vite.
>
> LE VIEUX, à la Dame: Vous m'excusez, Madame! Un in-
> stant! Va vite chercher des chaises!
>
> LA VIEILLE, à la Dame: —Je vous demande un petit moment,
> ma chère.
>
> THE OLD WOMAN to the Lady: A modest life, but a full one
> . . . Two hours a day, he works on his message.
> A bell is heard. Very shortly afterward the gliding
> noise of an embarkation was heard.
>
> THE OLD WOMAN to the Old Man: —Someone. Go quickly.
>
> THE OLD MAN to the Lady: Excuse me, Madame! An instant!
> Go get some chairs quickly.
>
> THE OLD WOMAN to the Lady: —I ask one small moment,
> my dear.[139]

What the old man says to the old woman, when both are on stage,
does not differ in setting from what both say to the Lady, who is
not there at all. Do we read manifestly in the direction of reality or
latently in the direction of fantasy? They themselves cannot ask

these questions: we are a step beyond Pirandello. And it is a crucial step. Within the framework of such a play, nothing latent or manifest is discernible (though the couple are manifestly there, the others not): reality resembles fantasy, fantasy resembles reality, and there is no language by which anyone, ourselves or the people in the play, can philosophize about this situation after the fashion of Pirandello's characters. The language by which one would do so would itself immediately illustrate the paradox.

The people in the play hope for an Orator, who is their Godot. And he does appear at the climax of the play, a dumb orator, who utters nonsense syllables. By appearing and speaking meaninglessly, he adds another dimension to the paradox of manifest appearance-latent nonappearance—that of meaning-meaninglessness. This paradox resides in the language, meaning or not: that of appearance or not resides in the staged action. But the action and the language are set to define each other, and in this impasse cannot come to definition. Language both recites action manifestly and uncovers it latently; thereby language *becomes* action. There is no definable result of the action, and the language does not move to a resolution. It is already *there*, in a total situation it continually illustrates and creates.

Or, to put it differently, there is such an unbridgeable distance between human action, as these modern plays conceive it, and human language, that the language of the character on stage cannot designate action completely enough to recite it, as on the imaginary stage of the Renaissance or the religious stage of the Greeks. Nor is the action seen in a stable framework of "reality," as in Ibsen and his successors, so that the language the character speaks may uncover the action. Rather, the distance between what is said and what is (or ought to be) done, in Beckett and Ionesco, is powerfully rendered through the tension between the two. The "modern predicament," in the abstract verbal structures of the stage, is envisioned by means of a procedure that implicitly questions those very structures, very much as the extreme literalness of film technique in certain directors

(Bunuel, Antonioni) pushes the emotions, of a geometry visual rather than primarily verbal, into an abstractness that seems unliteral; into a realm where terms like "realism" and "surrealism" have been superseded, and transcended.

But we have not only our modern predicament. In what Malraux calls our museum culture, we have all others as well: plays that recite over action and plays whose language uncovers action—Sophocles and Shakespeare as well as Ibsen and Chekov—are all equally accessible to us. Beckett and Ionesco suggest this too; and *Endgame* can be read for a comment on Shakespeare, as can Ionesco's redoing of the *Impromptu de Versailles* for one on Molière. They are, as we must be also, "literary"—at this pitch, the literary voice is not an evasion of the human but an especially intense way of embracing it.

: VI :

PERSON

When the language of a speaker is structured so as to generalize his actions, the speaker too tends to become generalized in his person: to become anonymous. As his words bend back on each other, he is bent back onto himself, and all questions of identity are subsumed in the unremitting abstractness of the way the spoken words, by which we would identify the personal nuances of a character, are forced into a syntax and signification within which identifications of person cannot take place. Kafka's protagonist in his novels, like Beckett's or Ionesco's in their plays, has been situated by the author in terms that render negligible his identification with any class of people less than mankind in general, including that class of one which consists of the author himself, who bears the initial of the character but has purged the character of incidental autobiographical resemblance (or difference).

As a limit of reference, Flaubert's finicky language, though it has an abstract side, operates to identify people, the lesson Maupassant learned from him: 'Describe this porter so he would be instantly recognizable among all the porters in the world.' If one carries the exactness of *Bouvard et Pécuchet* any farther, the "microscopic" level of *Ulysses* is arrived at, too detached for characterization, like fabric under a strong lens. That level, the stream of consciousness, abstracts into epiphanic, and generalized, series the points of a man's existence in such minute randomness that he cannot be identified as more than *l'homme moyen sensuel*. The details are too minute and too random to render a person; the epiphanic significance is too broad to be individualized.

Moreover, HCE, "here comes everybody," as he floats on the

current of a rendered dream, never is set into any coordinates which would either limit him or give him a mask or even constellate the mutiplicity of named persons whose roles he fulfills into a composite persona. The great generalities of Family and Conquest, Death and Consciousness, Sex and Guilt, rise to the surface as determinants of a whole life (Finnegan is dead) constantly recurrent (he revives).

Another direction of abstractness for the person is Proust's, whose search for an identity is posited on the search for the meaning of an abstraction, A la Recherche du temps perdu. The double-"I" redoubles, and comes out as more intensely single than an "I" whose coordinates would locate his person. Lacking the Flaubertian coordinates of being set by point of view in defineable relation to a fixed plot, Marcel, though ultimately he is of course central, cannot be called either central to the action exclusively or peripheral. Consequently, he cannot retrieve any identity from the plot more specific than the generalized person that it has, of course, been Proust's entire imaginative and linguistic strategy to bring into being. Marcel is central if one takes the action as its impingement on his consciousness; he is peripheral if one plots the action as happening by definition outside himself. He is central as universal, peripheral as unique. Rather, what he universalizes is the uniqueness of anyone.

Like Freud (whom he resembles in certain specific ideas), Proust presents a person who operates a double realm of unconsciousness-in-consciousness which makes his world more intensely single, a mystery which makes his identity evade his realization (it resides in the language of his definition from the outset) until the approaching anonymity of death. The approach of anonymity—the confusion by the younger generation in the final soirée at the points which place the aging guests—signalizes precisely the approach of personal annihilation, the formulation of the only possible personal definition and also of death.

This generalized person is post-Cartesian, insofar as the existence of self-conscious cerebration, instead of solving a philosophical problem, constantly generates an insoluble one. Again, an existential epistemology, Sartre's *pour-soi* and *en-soi* or Heidegger's *Situation,* translates the problem into a set of coordinates which are more ramified than the literary ones, and yet simpler, insofar as they only suggest the kind of person the works that parallel them fulfill: one could enrich Sartre by referring to Beckett's Hamm, but Sartre's language offers a structure elaborate in its remoteness from Hamm, or Marcel, subdividing in terminology what the play or the novel has managed to unify. Still again, *Geworfenheit* or *mauvaise foi,* sufficient as terms of abstract analysis, become insufficiently superficial characterizations of the splendidly generalized acts of the person in Beckett or Proust.

Or to put it positively, the generalized person in these modern works provides a literary, and therefore immediate, correlative to the transcendental Ego of Husserl, the *Man* of Heidegger. As in those philosophers, a plenitude of perception both enriches and neutralizes the self, so that the question of individuating character, like the related question of subject and object, has been removed. The result is a capacity for coping with a totality of experience, for trusting the phenomenological flow of perception in the philosophers, of language in the writers. The generality of the person is not to be seen, however, as a deprivation of individuality. As Heidegger says—and it takes such close-knit constructs as his to discuss this elusive question with any adequacy—"The *real being of a self* does not reside in an exceptional condition for the subject, freed from the generalized person; rather, *it is an existential modification of the generalized person as of something that is an essential Existential entity.*" (Das *eigentliche Selbstsein* beruht nicht auf einem vom Man abgelösten Ausnahmezustand des Subjekts, sondern *ist eine existenzielle Modifikation des Man als eines wesenhaften Existenzials.* [Italics Heidegger's])[140] "But then," he immediately reminds us, "The selfhood of a really existing Self is divided ontologically through a gap from the identity of an ego that maintains itself in

the manifold of experience." (Die Selbigkeit des eigentlich existier-
enden Selbst ist aber dann ontologisch durch eine Kluft getrennt
von der Identitaet des in der Erlebnismannigfaltigkeit sich durch-
haltenden Ich.)

In modern poetry, where the phenomenological flow of language
comes through most triumphantly, the pressure for generality shows
also as a pressure toward displaying a complexity for the internal
structure of the person imagined as speaking the poem. The simplified and generalized person of Beckett or Kafka is never arrived at
in poetry; the poeticized language does not permit such an arrival,
which would be a dead-end for its internal monologue. So transparent a style as Robert Creeley's crystallizes around an identity
whose internal structures are offered precisely for the revelatory profundity residing in the fact that their definitions do not come together. The person, though neutral, is multiple in "For a Friend."

> Who remembers him also, he thinks
> (but to himself and as himself)
>
> *Himself* alone is dominant
> In a world of no one else.

In fact, the transparency of the style allows the complexity to be
the more apparent, undistracted by any concretions. The multiple
self (not necessarily to be divorced from the poet's person, any more
than to be identified with it) traps into a further poetic definition
the bare abstractness of the linguistic gestures that would formulate it.

Language, as an act of self-consciousness, opens the possibility of
formulation; and through its indirectness as an instrument, it closes
that possibility, especially in poetry, which by definition must call
delightful attention to the indirectness and instrumentality of the
language it employs (to eschew indirectness, as Creeley in effect
pretends to do, itself posits directness as a higher form of indirect-

ness: tropes move toward a plenitude of "straight" syntax, the highest rhetoric not being multiple flourishes but the rhetorical effect in the absence of all rhetorical devices).

Language, for the knower of the self, serves as a kind of trap, and also as a kind of instrument, the only one at his disposal. As soon as a self-awareness objectifies itself into words, the words stand with their own syntactic order, their own associations, out and away from the self and its awareness. In poetry, the virtual and arbitrary character of this order itself enters into the statement. In classical poetry, as in ordinary language, this "otherness" of statement does not present a problem because no question is asked about it. Modern poetry does pose such questions. The ambivalent character of the trap-instrument language moves to the fore and demands itself to be incorporated into the poem.

In poetry that tries to be self-conscious, or in much poetry since Romantic times, the self speaking the poem becomes conscious of the self that speaks the poem. *The Prelude* sets out the "growth of a poet's mind." On the one hand, thereupon, the poem sounds the depths of the self, once it becomes full of feeling enough to mirror self as well as nature, to be not *naiv*, in Schiller's terms, but also *sentimentalisch*. "The poem," Schlegel says, "is a *higher* or a *deeper* I that frees itself from the I, the square root of I."[141] ("Das Gedicht ist ein *höheres* oder *tieferes* Ich das sich aus dem Ich ablöst—$\sqrt{Ich}$." [Italics Schlegel's])

But on the other hand, the person gets somehow fragmented into the particularities which he identifies himself with in the "negative capability" for which only a romantic poet could have found a name. Whitman excites himself in a long, sweeping line of fiat-by-incantation, to identify his self *(Song of Myself)* with anything he perceives, names, and captures. The essential act is the conceiving, preliminary one, at once poetic and moral, of giving himself a free rein (rhythmically also) to canvass whatever diversities occur to him.

The poet is then caught, once he moves his person to the fore, between a special way of knowing his person, and an impossibility in the way of knowing. Rimbaud sees this clearly, gives it a Cartesian contradiction (*je pense*), and deplores the anonymity inherent in the negative capability that Keats had—albeit in passing—welcomed:

> C'est faux de dire: je pense. On devrait dire: On me pense.
> Pardon du jeu de mots.
> Je est un autre. Tant pis pour le bois qui se trouve violon, et nargue aux inconscients . . .[142]

> It is false to say: I think. One ought to say: one is thought.
> Pardon the play on words.
> I is another. Too bad for the wood which finds itself a violin and sneers at the unaware . . .

"Je est un autre." Indirectness is inescapable, because it resides in the linguistic act.

It resides also, Valéry[143] says, in the irreconcilable multiplicity of entities we perceive when we perceive ourselves, our own bodies. Even seen simply (Valéry's title says *simple*), the body is three bodies, all of them indirect: the first body is a number of parts unrelated to one another, as the left hand feels the right alien to it if it holds it and the elbow has nothing to do with the back. The second, the body seen by others, no man who had not experienced the indirectness of the mirror could even recognize. The third, the physiological body, only reaches formulation after a series of complicated experimental operations in a language "more indecipherable than Etruscan texts. . . ." To unite these three bodies, Valéry posits a fourth, which he says is "absurd," and stops.

Intellection in his writing becomes depersonalized and disembodied, M. Teste. Or reflects on its body through the mediation of a mythological figure, Narcisse. The fullest "Narcisse" of Valéry is "Fragments du Narcisse," in which the speaker moves toward the limit of talking about the self as loving the self, caught in a void between intellections (the statements of the poem) and a physical situation (the speaker's body). The reflection, physical and intellectual, must break to frustrate the union, as it does in the lines given as the last:

> L'insaisissable amour que tu me vins promettre
> Passe, et dans un frisson, brise Narcisse, et fuit . . .[144]

Caught in a perceptual structure of indirection, the person of the self resists the identification most desired. Moreover, like perception, language, as an abstraction of naming and also as a selector from total reality, does retain its own indirectness, and loses the identification in the very act of formulating it, a Narcissus whose love is "insaisissable." The desire carries with it a hope of fulfillment for the "moi" which would make its pitfalls no longer "haissable."

The hope of unifying the self, as it presses language, issues in the simplified single person of the anonymous and generalized self, HCE and Hamm; or else it grapples with the multiplicities of indeterminate states within the speaking self, between the vaporization and the centralitzation of the Baudelairean "moi." Kafka takes the first alternative, and testifies to the release of abstraction in otherness when he says he first felt himself to be a writer when he switched from the first to the third person. Musil by his title announces the anonymity of a character whom a transparent and neutralizing style keeps from getting enmeshed in the concretions of rendered Viennese life: the man without properties, "Der Mann ohne Eigenschaften." Beckett in his trilogy opts for the second alternative and multiplies indistinguishably the faces of a speaker who can at the same time be presumed to be single. Malloy dissolves into Malone, Malone into Macmann, Sapo and Saposcat, Lambert and Lemuel; and all into the *Unnameable*. Third person and first person cannot sort out the masks from the faces, the anonymities from the identities, when the shift from first person into third serves as the means for dissolving them one into the other.

The Mask would seem to offer a way of combining the first alternative of generalized abstraction and the second of structured multiplication. Yet, once a mask is chosen, the distance of what is selected from its object is announced in the thing selected: the Mask posits a face to speak through it (*per-sona*), self or anti-self structured by the instrument of representation.

Captivated by the theory of the mask, Yeats resisted its oversimplification by inventing a spectrum for making a whole person totally responsive to external change, the phases of the moon. While he conceived of the person theoretically as a dynamic union of opposites, self with anti-self, his attempt to codify the person in "A Vision" quickly fragments the self into multiple faces: *Will, Mask, Creative Mind,* and *Body of Fate*—and *Mask* itself is subdivided into two masks, the false and the true. In the masks of his poems, Yeats tends to shift his *personae* from section to section of a poem, letting each hardened singleness of mask make only a partial, and coherent but fragmentary, statement. For the lover in the poem "Masks," indirection is necessary to fulfillment; he will not obey when asked to "put off that mask of burning gold/ With emerald eyes," lest love be destroyed in the process. In "A Dialogue Between Self and Soul," the Self answers the questions and allegations of the Soul by the indirection of dwelling on something other in space and in time, an "emblematical" ancient Japanese sword. Free of the dialogue in the second part of the poem, Self reverts to flux, "A living man is blind and drinks his drop." The person of the poem ends in an anonymous identification that has added just this step of generalization from the Wordsworthian self before concluding the poem in Wordsworthian praise:

> We are blest by everything,
> Everything we look upon is blest.[145]

The mask then, points up and focuses but does not resolve the multiplicities into which the person, under the pressure of self-questioning, finds himself fragmented when out of the flux of experience one bit is structured and then another bit. Behind the mask stands always the face. Once a writer has raised the question of identity, to present a mask, while it does confect an identity, at that very point raises the further question of how the mask relates to the face. This relation is felt, often, as a version of the other question, how one bit in the flux relates to another bit.

"La Jeune Parque" is the title, the mask, Valéry put to a poem which began as disconnected lines of verse. The subject remained what it was from the outset, a dramatized attempt to fix and relate the flux of psychological transformations. "Remember," he says of the finished poem, "That the true subject of the poem is the depiction of a series of psychological substitutions, and in brief the transformation of a consciousness ('le changement d'une conscience') over the duration of one night."[146]

Given the fragments, the "broken bundle of mirrors," (Pound) that the multiple self formulates and states itself to be feeling, the desire to unify these fragments in a poem may try to melt the mask into the face by presenting the tension of their disunion. Eliot's Tiresias is "throbbing between two lives," those of the immediate passage being a day life and a night life, but also the several lives of *personae* who are conceived of as melting into the figures of the Grail Legend, a melting that is merely assumed and therefore poses a perennial problem of understanding (of exegesis). The failure of Gottfried Benn's "Ikarus" concerns not the failure of Icarus' flight, but his failure to know himself in the vagueness of a swooning, prior rumination. The failure of consciousness includes as well as foreshadows the ultimate failure of act. Rilke's Orpheus eludes identity with the Greek figure, or the German poet, or the generalized reader. The generality of the command "Sei immer tot in Eurydike" (Be ever dead in Eurydice) addresses itself to an intimate second person who may be taken for any one of the three by himself, or any one identified with one of the others (reader with dying Orpheus, etc.).

Between the confected singleness of a mask and the irreducible multiplicity of the face, Laforgue suspends a resolution by sustaining an irony that reflects not on some part of the subject matter but on the (itself ironic) stance of a posed speaker. Irresolution is staged, and that which stages the irresolution, the irony, also occasions it.

The subject aired is the instrument of airing. Since the intellect comes in for raillery as, and because, the speaker reduces himself to using it, a process comparable to the process of dialectic is kept in motion. While the tone remains single, the stable point of view with constant agility pretends to threaten its own stability. Still, Laforgue avoids the neutral tone of intellectual self-perplexity. He mocks the intellect while using it, and thereby projects, in desperation about knowing the self, an insouciance before the desperation.

The self contrives a mask: Pierrot. The mask then elaborates on the self in a "Complainte" for employing intellection to hinder and not aid self-realization. The world is called imperfect, and then a second thought introduces the suspicion that it seems that way because the self is imperfect, initiating an unending process. Not the candle of "mon ami Pierrot" is dead, as in the lightly parodied folk song, but his brain, "ma cervelle est morte." The play out of and into self-conscious intellections enters the music of the poem, which abandons the direct, and hence purportedly unconscious, rhythm of the folk song at the very moment when it invokes "the unconscious," in alexandrines self-consciously abstract enough already to seem to anticipate those of Valéry:

> Ma cervelle est morte.
> Que le Christ l'emporte!
> Béons à la Lune,
> La bouche en zéro.[147]
> Inconscient, descendez en nous par réflexes:
> Brouillez les cartes, les dictionnaires, les sexes.

> My brain is dead.
> Christ take it off!
> Gape at the moon,
> The mouth a nought.
> Unconsciousness, come down to us in reflexes,
> Mix up dictionaries, maps, and sexes.

The determinations that coordinate experience in space (maps), in language (dictionaries), and in the physical and emotional distinctions of sex, are supposedly to be mixed up at the very moment the unconscious takes over. The clown who invokes the unconscious dominates the mixup all the while, because he constantly makes much of occupying the stage, of the fact that it is a stage he occupies. The speaker's brain is both dead and a hindrance ("Que le Christ l'emporte!"). The "inconscient" summoned along the route of the "réflexes," is not really supposed to help: it is chaos the speaker invokes. Or ironically invokes, driven to "desperation" by the state of the world (a fine place this is, to make me want its guides confused, its maps and dictionaries!) and also by the state of the self (the brain doesn't help; consequently I call on the unconscious, if only to mix things up when its reflexes take over). The mildness of the clown's irony corresponds to, and yet mitigates, the depth of the self-induced and "complained" plight. The irony turns, in the next couplet, back to the self, for a solution which will solve no more than some religious trickster might, an Indian fakir:

> Tournons d'abord sur nous-même, comme un fakir!
> (Agiter le pauvre être, avant de s'en servir.)
>
> Let's turn at first on ourself, like a fakir!
> (Agitate the poor being before using it.)

To begin with the self is to disturb the self, and the strangely displaced "we" of the self begins with itself ("d'abord") as a fakir does. To think is to escape feeling, to feel is to destroy the coordinates of thought. The self turns on itself, clowns in the mask of pretending to do so by (actually) only gaping at the moon. It's the world that's awry; so the poem's most succinct couplet claims:

> Tiens! l'Univers
> Est à l'envers . . .

Laforgue's irony, in the constant rebound of its throwback on the self, keeps exercising its acrobatics on the high wires of its own construction, never descending to the ground of a stable reference. Classical irony depends on a stable conception at the outset. "It's a fine day," as an ironic statement means "it's a bad day," with refer-

ence to the stable conception of what a fine day is. (The irony, if
spoken by an Eskimo, would be lost on a Dyak.) Pope's irony about
the literary world in *The Dunciad* and elsewhere depends on a
stabilized conception of what literature, and what the social status
of the writer should be. Even Byron's romantic irony depends on a
conception similarly stable: the shabby world is treating the writer-
hero badly. *Don Juan* shuttles between two stable conceptions of
the double standard, a stable idea of what chastity is, and a stable
notion that to flout chastity may involve quasi-heroic pleasure. In
Laforgue's irony no such stable conceptions exist, single or double.
The self has nothing to measure itself against, because the world
dissolves into its apperceptions. It aches to measure itself, and a
consciousness of this ache constitutes the special plight of the poet,
a surrogate for a humanity still learning about itself ("jeunes gens"):

> C'est pourquoi je vivotte, vivotte,
> Bonne girouette aux trent'-six saisons,
> Trop nombreux pour dire oui ou non . . .
> —Jeunes gens! que je vous serv' d'Ilote![148]
> > *(Avertissement)*

> That's why I eke my life, my life,
> Good weathercock with thirty-six seasons,
> Too numerous to say yes or no . . .
> —Young people! May I serve 's your slave.

The poet is drunk on his task (the last line alludes to the Spartan
custom of getting a helot drunk to show Spartan children what
drunkenness is). He points the direction, but too many ways for
affirmation or negation. The irony shuttles between one and another
of the thirty-six seasons, clear about not being clear, gay about being
sad. A Pierrot who is only a mask does not resume the person speaking; he only induces the sadness and near-perplexity of a self an-
nouncing ironically that after all Pierrot is only a mask. The next
poem in that series, "another complaint" ("Autre Complainte de
Lord Pierrot"), shows the speaker adopting his perplexity as an

amorous gambit in a courtship dialogue, using the self after agitat-
ing it . . .

Once again, irresolution is staged, and stagey. The mask becomes
an improvisation of language, a *"locution."* What, he asks or feigns
to ask, is the guiding spirit ("faculté-maîtresse") of the beloved who
has escaped from Pierrot's snares ("Locutions des Pierrots, II")?
To know this well is stated as the only end of his self-questionings:

> A seule fin de bien savoir
> Quelle est sa faculté-maîtresse![149]

The definition, then, is ironically collapsed into the *fact* of possession: to belong to him, the mistress says, is the "faculté-maîtresse."
(And still another irony; it is the faculty, a cerebral power of sorts
or even a *réflexe*, that is the mistress.) This condition sends the
masked Pierrot back round, in an unending circle, to the question
of how he can be certain of the self behind the mask when uncertainty about the self led him to don the mask:

> —C'est d'être la mienne, dis-tu?
> Hélas! tu sais bien que j'oppose
> Un démenti formel aux poses
> Qui sentent par trop l'impromptu.

> It is to be mine, you say?
> Alas! you know well that I oppose
> A formal denial to the poses
> That smell too much of the impromptu.

Pose and impromptu: a mask of the *face* itself? He denies this. And
"poses" is in the plural. The denial is merely formal. Moreover it
is ironic for that poet to deny the impromptu (denying the self as
a desperate courtship gesture for self-fulfillment) who has Pierrot
"free-associate" in poem after poem, who for example paints an
"Aquarelle en Cinq Minutes"—of Hamlet and Ophelia! A posing
Pierrot stalemates himself in pretending to refuse the poses of a
mistress to whom he "nourishes" a "divine attachment." Irony re-

leases the stalemate: denial of impromptu is itself denied by the fact that the denial itself improvises. And Pierrot just makes the flourish of this *locution* as one among many others; it sorts with his mask to make flourishes; he soon sweeps off to another.

The mask serves as a prop for the irony; a confected self probes and pretends to respond to the mysteries of the real self, which remain mysteries in the nonchalance of the mask-donning speaker presented "in the act" of donning a mask.

Since the speaker distracts himself and disclaims himself, the perception of self diffuses into the tone of the poem and sidesteps all the fixities of naming anything but the mask, "Pierrot." In the last poems that name itself is dropped, and the tone intensifies. Laforgue has the self meditate under three mysteriously indeterminate voices ("Le Mystère des Trois Cors"), or in a monody of solitude under the moon, a "Solo de Lune." In "Solo," "je" begins by facing the sky and ends with a nonsense metaphor about the frills of the beloved's skirt. This irony of anticlimax enters at the outset: the self dies and is at the same time merely jostled on top of a coach whose names signify a span from royalty ("impériale") to mere dutifulness ("diligence"):

Je fume, étalé face au ciel,
Sur l'impériale de la diligence.
Ma carcasse est cahotée, mon âme danse
Comme un Ariel;
Sans miel, sans fiel, ma belle âme danse,
O routes, coteaux, ô fumées, ô vallons,
Ma belle âme, ah! récapitulons.[150]

I smoke, stretched out facing the sky
On top of a coach.
My carcass is jostled, my soul dances
Like an Ariel;
Without honey, without venom, my fine soul dances,
O routes, slopes, O smokes, O valleys,
My fine soul, ah! let's recapitulate.

Immersed in the jouncing of the coach and in the landscape as he recapitulates a story of "exile" from love, the self posits the detachment of an historian, "without honey or venom," reversing, and muting, Tacitus' *sine ira et studio*. The reminiscence of Tacitus' savage irony gives a scale to the mildness of this irony. "Without sentiment, without satire," but sentiment and satire, honey and venom toward self and the world, are the two main constituents of this "solo." As always, they cannot be disentangled, there is no self to disentangle them. The body—slangily mocked for its mortality as a "carcasse"—is jostled, and the soul dances. The soul is summoned ironically, "ma belle âme," in a bittersweet of satire-become-sentiment, of intellect submerged in the act of feeling by a self posing only momentarily as a pure literary creation of spiritual flight: "Comme un Ariel." And "actually" he is left with nothing but the friendship of hotel rooms: "je n'ai que l'amitié des chambres d'hôtel,"[151] a letdown that occasions the poem, from which improvisation provides at once agony and release. A step further into improvisation and we would have the free-floating self in problematic union with its casual and transitory experience: "Tu es la nuit dans un grand restaurant." You are the night in a grand restaurant, or else you are in a great restaurant at night. In Laforgue, as here in Apollinaire's "Zone," the identity of the self begins to merge with the location of the self, and irony for Laforgue, a shift of tone for Apollinaire, sustains itself by resubmerging the self in its imagined location.

Not wholly, and the coordinates of existential *situation* cannot be mapped. The soul is free, the body is free, the self is free: they improvise together, and Laforgue reconciles himself to not deciphering the music they make in this "Solo." When the self recedes so persistently, recapitulation takes the form of divagation. At the same time, recapitulation is mocked by divagation as being impossible. Yet the poem poses no such paradox, for the self cannot resolve into one, being suspended in the freedom of a sustained irony whose intellections are angled so as only to graze the question.

Retaining the freedom of this ironic gesture is a tremendous poetic feat, the achievement of which can be apprehended by a look at Eliot's simplified version in the quasi-Laforguean "Love Song of J. Alfred Prufrock." Irony itself does not suffice, and Eliot falls far short of Laforgue's quizzical self, verging throughout on the simplification of Tennysonian nostalgia. "Prufrock," in fact, is the sort of dramatic monologue à la Browning that Tennyson might have written had he read Laforgue. We know exactly the position of Eliot's Prufrock, what he falls short of, how he falls short. His world in its way is as fixed as that of Pope's Belinda. For Eliot satire serves almost as an end; for the delicacy of Laforgue's "je" it is only a means.

Another measure of the poetic dexterity in Laforgue's staged irresolution is his attainment of a balance and affirmation far beyond the stridency of Mayakovsky, whose "I" in the poem of that title ("Ya") sets forth a self in metaphors of Laforguean extravagance without the Laforguean profundity. Mayakovsky stands between Byron and Apollinaire, but a shade closer to Byron. The irony toward self in "The Backbone Flute" and "The Cloud in Trousers" exhibits a verve and lightness that might be mistaken for profundity. A vague man (cloud) dressed up for poetic occasion (in trousers), Mayakovsky does little more than spruce up a standard romantic self with the formal flair of free verse. It takes, perhaps, a Pasternak to discern in this poet one who "chose the pose of external integrity. He kept this pose so completely that it is hardly possible to give the characteristics of its inmost secret."[152]

If Mayakovsky reached that point in his life—of which Pasternak is actually speaking—he did not do so in his poems. Still, the tension between life and poems (about life) does at least begin to get aired in Mayakovsky, and we might dwell on that side of his poems did we not have available the flights of that far more agile person, Apollinaire.

In his work the poem depends on the life as the mask does on the face; each inseparable from the other, and yet unidentifiable through any prestidigitation. A poem must somehow concern itself with life, as it must ultimately be in (a signifying) language and so have some kind of speaker. Instead of staging irresolution as Laforgue does, Apollinaire orchestrates a surge of resolve derived from a person who embraces the multiplicities of his face. The only mask he confects is the mask of an improvising self who tries to close the gap between the poem and life by pretending that the poem is not a way of seeing only, but a way of doing.

He "willfully" exhibits himself as inventing the poem, in "Zone," and even in the more formal "Les Collines." The self-advertising poem is a step beyond the mere poem; its speaker brazens out the contradictions inherent in the indirection of his language from his selfhood. Classical rhetoric advertises its ornamentation; Apollinaire's poem, adopting classical rhetoric among other flourishes, advertises the very creation at the heart of the ornamentation. The signifying character of the language, though, resists an analogy to action painting: the poem stands not as a unique constellation of the poet's psyche at the moment (although that too), but as a trial balloon toward signifying the speaking self in some fully viable, generalizing and signifying form. A willful playfulness, in which the poet virtually advertises his choice of image, resides in the oddness of the one Apollinaire chooses to begin "Les Collines," two airplanes he (pretends he) sees in combat over Paris, identified with his past and his future. This image is, first of all, casual—a "happening." And the poet dramatizes its occurrence on his field of vision, the sleight by which he invests it magisterially with a range of association. As well as being casual and complex, the image blazons its otherness. One's past and one's future are abstract, and stored inside the self, not concrete and visible over a city: the differences between the person's past and future and two airplanes adds fuel to the imagined likeness: the imagination itself is celebrated, by implication here, as more explicitly at the end of the poem.

Even odder is the central image, the comparison of "great men" (of whom the poet self-mockingly proclaims himself to be one) to hills. Mock logic ("you see the future is in flames") dissolves too quickly in this ranging voice to function structurally, as it does in English Baroque poetry; the poet is "busy" proclaiming himself a prophet:

> Où donc est tombée ma jeunesse
> Tu vois que flambe l'avenir
> Sache que je parle aujourd'hui
> Pour annoncer au monde entier
> Qu'enfin est né l'art de prédire.[153]

> Where then has my youth fallen down
> You see the future is in flames
> Know that I am speaking today
> To announce to the entire world
> The art of prophecy at last is born.

This self has not yet dissolved into the irrational anonymity of surrealism; it has not taken the step of celebrating the collective unconscious, but insists on the integral character of the person, through, and not in spite of, the quasi-surrealistic multiplicity of its experience. The song is sung at top pitch; there are no notations of punctuation (a form of musical as well as logical notation) to channel it, only the bare formal lines. Whitman's fiat-by-celebration has been clarified through formalization; and Apollinaire likewise identifies himself, playfully rather than solemnly, with whatever the fluid person *says* he *sees*: the act of perception is deliberately fused with the act of language:

> Je m'arrête pour regarder
> Sur la pelouse incandescente
> Un serpent erre c'est moi-même
> Qui suis la flûte dont je joue
> Et le fouet qui châtie les autres[154]

> I stop myself to take a look
> Upon the incandescent grass
> A serpent strays it is myself

> Who am the flute on which I play
> And the whip that chastises others

Whitman's lounger is on the incandescent grass ("I pause and invite myself"); the poet's Pelagian self has become an innocent serpent, his prophetic music a flute, his satiric scourge a whip. Three contradictory images are merged here "easily" by free-association, by-passing the complexities of self-consciousness and its depths:

> Profondeurs de la conscience
> On vous explorera demain[155]

The consciousness exists not as a subject, but in action, not the imitated intellectual action of Laforgue, but a poetic, image-making action. The question of person comes up again and again, and it is bypassed again and again, as the open structure of the poem permits it to be: the dark is indicated by the fact that it is whistled in.

Since this poem is not in an irresolution about free-association, it permits the certitude of simple assertion. Since no particular stance is staged—the poet carries his staging folded under his arm—a great range of tone is permitted, a range that itself signifies the virtual integration in the self (the meter unifies the poem) above and beyond the momentary naming of violence, for example; or of the gentleness into which it can melt. So the poet compares his love to a hurricane that deracinates a shrieking tree; and then in the very next line directs an intimate second person—the self or the beloved or the reader—to see gentleness everywhere:

> Ainsi attaque ce que j'aime
> Mon amour ainsi l'ouragan
> Déracine l'arbre qui crie
>
> Mais vois quelle douceur partout[156]

The abrupt tonal shift from violence to gentleness tests, and proves, the expansiveness of the self, by showing the self as expanding be-

yond these particular limits. Apollinaire here dramatizes what Mayakovsky just bluntly states:

> I feel that my "I" is too small for me.
> Someone is obstinately breaking out of me.

Elements that as images and as moments of the self are fragmentary
and contradictory (serpent, flute, whip; hurricane, gentleness) get
swept up in the willy-nilly equivalence of paratactic syntax and
monodic line.

That this bravura carries its own absurdity also enters the poem:
Laforgue's irony has been displaced from the center to serve as a
qualifying undertone. The poem is spoken as a burning act of a life
that falls short of its aspirations: "Ils n'égalent pas leurs destins."[157]
The self is dramatized as "really"—not in the mask Pierrot or Prufrock—speaking on impulse; Apollinaire invents the sketch-poem, the
metered jotting on the back of a menu or a postcard. The letter-
poem or informal epistle is likewise his invention, and the doodle-
poem or *calligramme* (the name surely ironic). The poem comes in
a drunkenness ("Alcools") like the one in which he and André
Salmon shattered their glasses at the beginning of a friendship, "the
river that fertilized us all."

The poet revels in the multiplicity of the self, to the point of
absurdity, welcoming that point finally because it permits the "relief" of positing a resolution confidently acknowledged as make-
believe. It was only when he worked over the first draft of the poem
"Cortège" that Apollinaire could invent an initial image absurd
enough to float the gaiety of a self-knowledge gained by means of
its opposite, ignorance: a peaceful backward-flying bird who nests
in the air:

> Oiseau tranquille au vol inverse oiseau
> Qui nidific en l'air.[158]

This image, and the other indirect resources into which the poem moves, are declared necessary for illuminating the self, which he names, because it is sombre and dull when seen close up: "Et moi aussi de près je suis sombre et terne." The very gratuitousness of saying that he receives illumination from a nonexistent creature allows him a freedom of verbal motion great enough to join or leave the self at will, to mix the times (past, present and future) when the self is confronted:

> "Au point qu'il deviendra un jour l'unique lumière."
> Un jour
> Un jour je m'attendais moi-même
> Je me disais Guillaume il est temps que tu viennes
> Pour que je sache enfin celui-là que je suis
> Moi qui connais les autres
>
> To the point that it will become one day the sole light
> One day
> One day I was waiting for myself
> I was saying Guillaume it is time you came
> So I could know at least the one I am
> I who know others

The other is revelled in, multiplied, catalogued, as one of the poem's several definitions-by-distinction. The invented bravura of this procedure gives him imaginative room to culminate in the "suddenly discovered" subject of the poem, another absurdity which, like the backward-flying bird, entered the poem only in the gradual fulfillment of revision: a funeral *cortège* for the body that he "realizes" is his own. Those who follow the body reconstruct him like a tower; since, if he is others, then they are the pieces of himself:

> Tous ceux qui survenaient et n'étaient pas moi-même
> Amenaient un à un les morceaux de moi-même
> On me bâtit peu à peu comme on élève une tour

Death, the Other, the Self, the Body—all these abstractions become identified, but only impulsively in the playfulness of the poem. Perception starts a loving merry-go-round of past-present-future and self-other and death-life, the absurdity forcing the poem to a more and more rhythmic affirmation. It ends by leaving images behind it, in abstractions that the images have absurdly refreshed:

> Rien n'est mort que ce qui n'existe pas encore
> Près du passé luisant demain est incolore
> Il est informe aussi près de ce qui parfait
> Présente tout ensemble et l'effort et l'effet

> Nothing is dead but that which does not yet exist
> Next to the shining past tomorrow is colorless
> It is without form, too, beside the perfect thing
> That presents at a stroke both effort and effect

Nothing is dead (so the poet, of course, is not really dead, as he bows offstage by cryptically admitting). Nothing, that is, except in the future, dead because it lacks form and color. In calling the past perfect, the poet, in his new role of couplet-philosopher, invokes a tautological pun: perfect signifies that which is past as well as that which is complete. In encountering his own past, he can unite striving and achievement (effort and effect). But he is not his past. The resounding climax crosses the line into an absurdity no less than that of the backward-flying bird or the man present at his own funeral. But because conclusions can be no more than intuitively provisional in this advancing life where self mingles with the others who abandon it, the poet may brave the absurd aphorism as he does the absurd image. The poem can string together backward-flying bird, funeral procession, and abstractions, with no more justification than that these are the formulations that "easily" come to hand. There is an irony of self-deprecation implied, a super-Laforguianism. "While waiting through the unending time till the language of defining persons gets formulated, I will revel in these fireworks of real and make-believe, life and corpse, self and others, present past and future. The flash of the fireworks will light up the terrain momentarily—all that can be hoped for, and gaily indulged, in the undeplored absence of a sun."

Apollinaire enters exuberantly into indirectness of language to get at the indirectness of the self's knowledge of itself. The multiplicity inherent in varied emotional states is not described, or tentatively structured, but "simply" indulged. Now there is a system of intellectual analysis by which the indirectness of what emotional states mean is described and structured—Freudian analysis. Still, the language of Freudian terminology mediates technically between the self and its stances—too technically for its vocabulary to be adopted directly for poetry. The Freudian poems of French and American poets that exhibit or name the unconscious—surrealist poems—siphon the self off in a simplistic anonymity that loses all the tensions Apollinaire manages to exploit. For these a poem worthy of comparison with Laforgue or Apollinaire ought to find some substitute beyond a mere vocabulary or image-formula.

And by using a Freudian perspective, Robert Lowell does manage to help close the gap between the self and its stances; he accepts the Freudian components as the given components of the poem, so much given that they would be redirected to be labelled. *Life Studies* suggests the internal dynamism of the self through a bare presentation of loaded facts. The manifest content of what is done or remembered, and the latent content of unconscious motive, are fused by the linear and unrhetorical progress of the poem, creating the central illusion: when the latent is thrust forward in this way so as to dominate evenly whatever proceeds, then the waking world, for all its rationality, may appear to be as unconscious as the world of dream, and without any recourse to surrealist irrationality. The person, like the narcissistically circular self of Norman O. Brown's *Life Against Death*, defines himself by every choice and gesture as dominated by sublimations (which need not be called that). These sketches—"life studies"—are taken of a model who offers only the lines of the unconscious, because the details, in crying out for significance, get it only from the Freudian unconscious. The soberness of the verse narrative in what might be called couch-pastoral, resists all gestures which would take it from the central "couch-oriented" introspection.

The "I" of the poem "merely" remembers and recounts. He and his wife lie on the mother's bed, "literally and figuratively," one might say; except that here literally *is* figuratively, so much so that verbal similes and metaphors enter these poems initially for their primitive job of Homeric explanation, having no figurative or vehicular function beyond that of any single detail in the poem. Similes cannot figuratively expand a world that is already totally figurative, or give imaginative cast to a self that sets its limits wholly in what it imagines and projects under the domination of the unconscious. Career and thought, history and nature, are here subordinated to the progression of Freudian remembrance, and so to the contour of the remembering self. Death and love, traditional subjects for Romantic and other lyric poetry, become once again the lyric subjects, now tempered crucially by Freudian references. Death is what the once infant boy remembers as striking his mind first at a time before entering the Freudian stage of latency. It is significant for him, rather than exactly a piece of wisdom—the significance cannot be summed up because it circles back on himself—when he now remembers the death of a dying uncle, "My Last Afternoon with Uncle Devereux Winslow."[159] That first death, in the order of *Life Studies*, precedes those of the father and mother: the greater Freudian significances are drawn toward in stages. The child, dawdling in the wings as the dying uncle enters toward the end of the poem, is said to be not a child—that is, to exist already fully in the light of sublimated significances; to be the imperially corrupt, imprisoned "mother," of an already androgynous world:

> I wasn't a child at all—
> unseen and all-seeing, I was Agrippina
> in the Golden House of Nero. . . .

The tactile and visual sensations of the immobilized child get swept up, for the poem, in the perception of this Death:

> My hands were warm, then cool, on the piles
> Of earth and lime,
> a black pile and a white pile . . .

> Come winter,
> Uncle Devereux would blend to the one color.

The familial context, remembered analytically, composes into a scene whose depths become those of the remembering poet's feelings. Mere deliberate naming functions to set up perspectives on these depths, because the deliberateness has been put through a transforming process largely in the tone and rhythm but also in the angle of approach to the subject matter. It is significant of the *poet*, as always, that his aunt refused all suitors, for her music; that he dredges up the memory of her combined eating and reading in her narcissistic bed. The self is a distant self, the remembered child, manipulated through the events of the poem by a composing process that renders a near self. This process resembles a psychoanalysis in indirection, but not in final signification. Where the clinical act envisages cure, this poetic process implies a universal condition. The meanings are never tagged on, summed up, or structured, because they may be presumed to exist "already" in every detail; and still the organization of the poem stands a step beyond a case study just because it has limited itself to the "raw materials" that life presents for study:

> Up in the air
> by the lakeview window in the billiards-room
> lurid in the doldrums of the sunset hour,
> my Great Aunt Sarah
> was learning *Samson and Delilah*.
> She thundered on the keyboard of her dummy piano
> with gauze curtains like a boudoir table,
> accordionlike yet soundless.
> It had been bought to spare the nerves
> of my Grandmother,
> tone-deaf, quick as a cricket,
> now needing a fourth for "Auction,"
> and casting a thirsty eye
> on Aunt Sarah, risen like the phoenix
> from her bed of troublesome snacks and Tauchnitz classics.

The sunset, the romantic landscape in general, the upper-class game, the silent music of the Biblical opera sublimating an aunt's erotic urges—these fairly traditional subjects are themselves reduced to the status of elements in the sketches of other people, present only for the reason that they stand in an emotional relation to the poet, a relationship Freudian because familial and eventful because remembered.

The composition is basically freer in its transitions, though less diffuse in emotional tone and overall range, than Apollinaire's "Zone." The tone, in fact, is quite strict. The deliberation of this voice moves in a pressure that isolates the details line by significant line. Under the totality of his own sublimation (represented by the poem itself) the pitch of the poet is locked tight to the point where it cannot insist because every detail is insistence. That being the case, the tone cannot vary a jot. The poem moves ahead with the even, ritual slowness of a funeral procession. Self and other need not be enigmatically joined and sundered because they are already one in the dominations to which the remembrance of the speaker testifies. He would characteristically remember those aspects of Aunt Sarah's likeness to himself. The unconscious has been brought out into the open, not through analysis, but by a "conscious" marshalling of significant details. The multiplicity of the self gets subsumed in a virtual unity by leaving the problem of the self as a problem more remote than the poem, or its implied notion of human language, could approach.

Put differently, it is the masks that are multiple, not the faces here: and this strategy turns the tables on the normal one, creating the poetic illusion that the face can be simple. The rationalism of the language in these poems serves very much the way irrationalism does for the surrealist, as a bridge between anonymity and identity. And more so. Identity becomes the mere uniqueness of the random series of relationships for a self; unique in series, relationships possess a functional significance that is the same for everybody: one must pass through the Freudian anonymity, poetically as well as clinically, the poet implies, in order to achieve identity. The person moves, and the poem pretends to fix the moving person in some stable order of words. For Lowell, the stable words are themselves, implicitly, produced by the flux of sublimations. Flux never comes in for naming, as it does under the manipulations of Laforgue and Apollinaire ("La vie est variable, aussi bien que l'Euripe"), who make it a structural element and an abstraction, while it serves Lowell as a principle.

One of the fluxes to which the poet, as a moving person, must be subject, is his own changes of language. René Char, after he abandons the strategies of an almost straight surrealism, makes the flux of the poet's attention to the language at hand the principle on which the poems themselves function. This holds for his whole work, and also for the parts of it, whose relations he effectually reorders by adding marginalia to them as well as by printing them with additional poems. When he is in love, he writes love poems, full of a rich surrealist imagery as a way of exemplifying that particular flux (and not only as a way of testifying to amorous exuberance). When he returns to the theory of poetry, he does not build poems that follow the theory, but rather makes the theory the subject of the poem, a formal sharing, *Partage Formel*. In the sleep of a war, fighting under a pseudonym for the underground, the poet turns his poems into a series of notes, the leaves of a man whose pseudonym is the sleeper, *Feuillets d'Hypnos*.

The subject of the poems, and their form, are made to seem dictated by the situation of the poet's person at that point in his flux, a situation reflected "directly" in the poems through an Apollinairesque feigned insouciance (feigned out of, and with reference to, a real insouciance about poetry when war is pressing).

Since life has dissolved into fragments, anecdote is at once adopted and severely criticized:

> (Prends garde à l'anecdote. C'est une gare où le chef de gare déteste l'aiguilleur!)

(Watch out for the anecdote. It is a station in which the
stationmaster hates the switchman!)

But Char sets this statement in parenthesis after an anecdote, and
the paradox it announces gets lost in the thickets of a metaphor that
on inspection will be found to be almost impenetrable. The anecdote itself has been set on the moving track of the poet's train of
thought, and not kept in the stability (station) of parable. The
anecdote may be used if it is thus watched out for? Or is the com-
mandment to beware absolute? We consult the collapsing metaphor, and end with the parenthesis closed, which declares the principle to be an afterthought and sends us either back, precisely, to
the anecdote it caps, or ahead to the next jotting in *Feuillets*.

The person is defined in aphoristic jottings, in the spurts of
metaphor, but only the particular aspect of the person who as a
poet has been involved by history in an urgent action, at a time when
identity must conceal itself as anonymity and the real person appear
in jots and spurts.

Again, the style changes completely, is made to change and testify
to the self in change, when Char "returns" to poetry after the war
that has pulverized poetry, to regrind his images and concentrate
on the art in *Le Poème Pulvérisé*. There even the war reminiscence,
like "Donnerbach Mühle," poses a self fully wakeful to a trans-
anecdotal circuit of poetic significances in the seemingly anecdotal
concrete situation around the self.

So glad is the newly awakened self that it appends new poems in
the form of notes to the "pulverized" poems, the *Arrière-Histoire
du poème pulvérisé*. These, in turn, use explanatory notes not really
to explain, in the delimited clarification of the note as a form, but
rather for a springboard into further leaps of the self. "Mon intention," he says about writing the *arrière-histoire* (and in it) "était
légère." His intention was light; he announces himself as an Apollinaire, which is to carry Apollinaire, who made no such announce-
ments, a step further. Poetry, he goes on to say, clear or opaque,

resembles life in being a mystery (so it does not matter whether the opaque "poème pulvérisé" is clarified by these notes):

> Quoique affaire terrestre, comme la vie dont elle est l'endroit victorieux du temps, claire ou opaque, la poésie reste un mystère.[159]

Although a terrestrial affair, a mystery. The poem never tries to resolve that mystery; it testifies to the poet's desire of resolution, a desire that remains in the state of desire, "désir demeuré désir." The self-triumph, over the self-contradiction, of the person is attained by keeping the poet moving past the contradiction, further and further; till finally, like the later Char, he can rest content with having later poems resemble earlier ones: to relax in the motion, in that context, is itself a form of motion; a stability of the dancer has become not inertness but a step in the dance.

The "person" of Char is single at any point; the multiplicity of the moving self is revealed in the motion from poem to poem, when the poems are looked at as a whole. And also, within the individual poem, the factitiousness and self-concealment of statement under an openness of tone as they appear in the paradoxes of a poem's images or syntax or sequence, generate a virtual multiplicity which the fresh language will not actualize. The generality of the individual poem operates to suggest a virtual multiplicity in the self of the speaker, by analogy to the paradoxes within a poem, of image or syntax or sequence. But the "direct" voice of the speaker will not allow that multiplicity to be more than suggested; he remains, thereby, (also) virtually single, moving on to a fresh, somewhat contradictory, statement before he can be crystallized into any multiplicities.

The person of Pound's *Cantos* is both multiple and moving; the notion of the face and its masks, instead of governing the shifts from short poem to short poem, has become the organizing principle of a very long one.

Within *The Cantos*, the fact that Pound declares the sections to be sections of the same poem allows him for that poem to enlist the flux of the self, an effect Char gains by manipulating the language of the individual poem. *A Draft of XXX Cantos* is permitted to retain its title and remain a draft, while at the same time being incorporated into the larger work that transmutes it. If Pound reads Chinese history, impelled to do so by the intention of writing cantos, then a long stretch of *The Cantos* is filled with bits from the particular Chinese history he reads, out of which certain image-event nubs are concatenated, selected but scarcely "digested." The exiled American returns to the letters of J. Q. Adams and Jefferson: the next Cantos compose mosaics of quotations from their letters. Pound is imprisoned at Pisa: and the person of the poet strips off his masks for reminiscences triggered by actual visual associations, the mountains and peasants he can see from his tent mingling with bits he hears or remembers. The shape of the *Pisan Cantos*, ruminative, sorrowing, and recapitulative, has become adaptively what the shape of time has dictated.

To see *The Cantos* as conversational improvisations (Blackmur, Tate) on the one hand, or on the other hand as some newer "rose-in-the-steel dust" version of a classical repetition-with-variation (Kenner), is to ignore the expansive interaction of the speaking self with what the self has thought over. The poet of *The Cantos* represents a person too mobile in his multiplicities to allow either for random fragmentation or for any sort of structured organization. When Kenner asserts that the *Rock-Drill Cantos* repeat, Canto for Canto, the themes of the first "Draft" Cantos, he has only chosen a particular facet of the generality in *The Cantos* so as to slant toward some special order the more complex seeming-order that the poem creates. Kenner's particular correspondences happen to hold. So do others, among other parts of *The Cantos*—correspondences with those same parts, and with others. The ideograms are only there, in space, the space of a page that sets them in some kind of relation; and in time, the time of the sequentially read, rhythmed poem that is constantly adaptive so as to salvage itself ("From the wreckage of Europe, ego scriptor") from the all-destroying time of history ("Time is the evil. Evil . . .").

Already in *Personae*, as the title indicates, Pound has sent his own voice (*per-sona*) through the lives of poets actual (Provençal, Chinese, Anglo-Saxon, Latin) or invented (Hugh Selwyn Mauberley). His own person lies behind the *persona*. The process of using another real life entails, of course, a selection from that life of matter appropriable for masking the living poet. As Pound early says, "I began this search for the real in a box called *Personae*, casting off, as it were, complete masks of the self in each poem. I continued in long series of translations, which were but more elaborate masks."[161] Sensitive to the dialectic of this process in *Personae*, Pound calls attention to it by restricting some poems to mere "translation." Others he builds along the lines of asking the strategic question about the process he is employing: how can one understand the flux of another life by looking back at details of it from a stable if adjustable point of view? A search for the real Bertram de Born organizes "Near Perigord," and the process of the search occasions the one coherent thread of comment through the poem. The search for the past breaks the confected persona into fragments, "a broken mirror of memory," in Kenner's phrase: the means toward composing the persona becomes also the instrument of discomposing it. In constructing "Near Perigord," Pound has deliberately put the fragments about Bertram together in such a way that they will never cohere. The woman with whom the poem ends abruptly has been introduced under Dante's epigraph about the schismatic Bertram, "And they were two in one and one in two" ("Ed eran due in uno, ed uno in due," *Inferno* XXVIII, 125):

> She who could never speak save to one person,
> And all the rest of her a shifting change,
> A broken bundle of mirrors. . . ![162]

Here, and in the "translation" poems, the language of the poet is modified by adopting into itself fragments not from the language of life but from other books, fragments that are kept from being assimilated or disguised beyond recognition in order that their second-handedness may function in the poem. When he uses other books this way, Pound is only making over for his own use a relation traditional since the Renaissance between the book and a person's self-knowledge. We use books to know the self, and introspection for us characteristically entails the roundabout process of going to something not within the self but outside the self, a book—in contrast to the medieval practises of spiritual discipline, which, however, themselves got codified in their later stages into such books as Ignatius' *Spiritual Exercises*. Montaigne's announced purpose was to know, in his own spirit, the human "esprit ondoyant et divers." To accomplish that purpose he went on no pilgrimage and entered no monastery, but instead shut himself up in a third-floor tower, a tower lined with books. Over the tower room he set a quotation not from the Word of God but from a Stoic philosopher. He gradually came to know himself by the indirect means of a mosaic of quotations, and the history of the three editions of the *Essais* is largely a history of fleshing out the meandering prose by a diversity of quotations. The trials of the self, the "essais," are made through books, and more books—fragments of books, as in Pound.

In the "translation" poems of *Personae*, such as "Homage to Sextus Propertius," Pound keeps entirely to the book; the antithesis between book and life when the book is about life is made to reflect the antithesis between self and other when the other is an admired poet. The term "homage" implies the distance between the face of the speaker and the severe mask he has adopted. The distance is also preserved by the fact that the translated quotations from Pro-

pertius are arranged into a pattern of Pound's own and are also
slanted in the direction of satire (Kenner's point) and of literary
precept—of directions, as it were, for doing what Pound is doing
when he follows the directions. The homage resides in taking Propertius as a "persona," the "persona" resides in performing translation as an homage. Not all Pound's translations are included in
Personae. Those that are included thereby gain this added dimension: they are called "personae."

This dimension expands in *The Cantos*. The Odysseus of Canto I
is not merely a Propertius-like persona for the poet whose personal
voice breaks out with the new theme and juxtaposed double-persona
of Canto II: "Hang it all Robert Browning/There can be but the
one Sordello." Canto I itself breaks away from translation before
the end, which "Homage" does not do. The recurrent and emerging
characters, Odysseus and Sordello, Malatesta and Adams, Confucius
and the Chinese emperors, the god Dionysus and Dante himself,
stand to the verbal acts of the multiplied Pound-self as the multiple
quotations stand to the invented words of the poem. Personae-
fragments appear in blocs, like the ideograms with which they sometimes merge. In *The Cantos* Pound has managed to bring together
two techniques to which he devoted prolonged study, the technique
of the persona, and the "imagistic" technique of the ideogram.

The ideogram has been correctly regarded as the structural principle basic to the Cantos, and to understand its function there as a
mirror for the person of the speaker, a close examination of its
linguistic technique, in Pound's usage, is required. What meets the
eye of the poet need not be a book; it may be something seen (as
a quotation can itself be levelled to the status of an image, something seen, or of an ideogram, a stylized presentation of something
seen. The Chinese quotations—as quotations, imaged pictograms at
times, and ideograms—resume all three.).

In his imaginative beginnings Pound applies himself to endowing
the visual image with a precision that is so elusive as to suggest some
vagueness quite contrary to precision. In his famous image about

the Metro, Pound acts almost as though he were a Rimbaud "fixing vertigoes":

> The apparition of these faces in the crowd:
> Petals on a wet, black bough.[163]

Or consider the function of the image in the following, far more elusive poem:

L'ART, 1910

> Green arsenic smeared on an egg-white cloth,
> Crushed strawberries! Come, let us feast our eyes.[164]

The visual precision here seems to be imitating a still-life, and the title seems to refer to something that could include a kind of painting. The relation between poem and title appears to be that between signifier and signified: arsenic-cloth-strawberries points to L'Art, 1910; pretends to be, indeed, a sort of ideogram for it. But when we inspect this seeming precision, it disappears into the vagueness of generality. We are left with a pure impression, as though Pound had reversed for a poem his dictum about the prose artist:

> Also there are various kinds of clarity. There is the clarity of the request: Send me four pounds of ten-penny nails. And there is the syntactical simplicity of the request: Buy me the kind of Rembrandt I like. This last is an utter cryptogram. It presupposes a more complex and intimate understanding of the speaker than most of us ever acquire of anyone. It has as many meanings, almost, as there are persons who might speak it. To a stranger it conveys nothing at all.
>
> It is the almost constant labour of the prose artist to translate this latter kind of clarity into the former; to say 'Send me the kind of Rembrandt I like' in terms of 'Send me four pounds of ten-penny nails'.[165]

If the Rembrandt statement is an "utter cryptogram," *L'Art* 1910, too, sets up its own cryptogram, pretending precision (the ten-penny nails kind of statement, at which "Imagism" aimed) in terms of generality (the Rembrandt statement).

In this little poem the visual side of the image is clear to the eyes that are invited to feast on it (egg and strawberry suggest food, as arsenic suggests an ingestible poison). The signification of the image, however, gets obscured in the generality of the title: "L'Art 1910" could stand for a moment in history, or else for a surrealist medley of all the arts taken together at a given moment of time. No mediation is possible between the visual clarity and the semantic obscurity: the meaning for which the text of the poem is an ideogram is utterly important in the poem and utterly inaccessible.

A comparable obscurity of signification, residing in a clarity of visual perception, is generated by the single images in *The Cantos*, from "Ecbatana" to "the gloom where the gold gathers the light against it." The single ideograms there, present to the eyes, seem to be mediated by the speaking person; it is he, in turn, whom they seem to be revealing by their mediation. But a circular process is really set up; we have the illusion that all the blocs in *The Cantos* can be read back and forth in the light of each other. Actually in their conjunctions they are as isolated from final signification of any classical sort as is the single image of "L'Art 1910." Indeed, since no one of them singly has a clearer signification than "L'Art 1910," they cannot be taken together for a Gestalt of signification. This brings us back to the self of the speaker, but he in turn merges with other selves, very much the way one image merges with other images. . . .

Each individual Canto is made up of blocs of statement, and each bloc tends to center in a visual perception (ideogram) or an event from someone's life (persona), or occasionally on something that possesses the dual character of ideogram and persona. Ideogram exists, then, "paratactically," on an absolute level with persona, so that one cannot be signifier and the other signified. Beyond the smaller blocs within *The Cantos*, each Canto itself constitutes a larger bloc, usually a persona, which is set off against other blocs: the Odysseus-bloc of Canto I sets off a Sordello-bloc in Canto II; the two set off a Cid-bloc; all set off a Dionysus-bloc, etc.

The movement from small bloc to bloc is adaptive, and "improvisational." The blocs can be long or short, as the numbered Cantos themselves may be. They respond, as they are posed, to the freedom of the "speaking poet." One need not end Canto XXIX to begin Canto XXX, since its bloc is set against the bloc of the other Canto. A "greater distance" does not hold always between Cantos than between sections within a Canto, because there is nothing but white space to measure the distance, and the self is all (multiple) one:

Glide of water, lights and the prore,   (1)
Silver beaks out of night,
Stone, bough over bough,
                    lamps fluid in water,
Pine by the black trunk of its shadow
And on hill black trunks of the shadow
The trees melted in air.

XXX

Compleynt, compleynt I hearde upon a day   (2)
Artemis singing, Artemis, Artemis
Agaynst Pity lifted her wail:
Pity causeth the forests to fail,
Pity slayeth my nymphs,
. . . [11 *lines about Pity*] . . .
In Paphos, on a day
                    I also heard: (3)
. . . goeth not with young Mars to playe
But she hath pity on a doddering fool,
She tendeth his fyre,
She keepeth his embers warm.

Time is the evil. Evil.   (4)
                    A day, and a day   (5)
Walked the young Pedro baffled,
                    a day and a day
After Ignez was murdered.

Came the Lords in Lisboa   (6)
                    a day, and a day
In homage. Seated there
                    dead eyes,

Dead hair under the crown,
The king still young there beside her.

Came Madame " ϒ ΛΗ   (7)
Clothed with the light of the altar
And with the price of the candles
"Honour? Balls for yr. honour!   (8)
Take two million and swallow it."[166]

A link of association moves us from one numbered section to another. But the link between the end unit of Canto XXIX (1) and
the long start of Canto XXX (2), *trees* and forests, is no less than
that between Pity (2) and the Venus-Mars (3) opposition; the
second link lies between Pity and the illustration of pity, but via a
change from Greece (Paphos) to Rome or a Renaissance view of
Rome (Mars).

So the link between (3) and (4), may be "doddering" and "time,"
though the links are not that set: the link may lie between "Pity"
and "time" by way of self-qualification: "Pity is the evil; or no,
Time is." The movement is temporal, a pure succession, "a day,
and a day," that links the love of Pedro I of Portugal for Ignez
da Castro (Canto III also), perhaps via Venus (3), with time (4),
and with his bafflement of Odysseus-like wandering after her murder (5).* And temporal succession continues, from the bafflement (5)
to his order, on ascending the throne, that his nobles do homage
to her corpse (6). This raises the question of form (loveable life)
and substance (the body) as related to love, a question already
dominating the bloc of Canto VII and now repeated by linking the
dead Ignez (5) with Aristotelian Substance, "Madame Hyle," per-
sonified after the fashion of medieval allegory, "Lady Philosophy,"
etc. (7). Death in time may (6) involve religion (7) which costs

---

*For the ideographic significance that may reside in a bare act, Pound's early
comment on Ignez is quite relevant: "The tale of Ignez will perhaps never be
written greatly, for art becomes necessary only when life is inarticulate and when
art is not an expression, but a mirroring, of life, it is necessary only when life is
apparently without design; that is, when the conclusion or results of given causes
are so far removed or so hidden, that art alone can show their relation. Art that
mirrors art is unsatisfactory, and the great poem, "Ignez da Castro," was written
in deeds by King Pedro. No poem can have as much force as the simplest narra-
tion of the events themselves."[167]

money, something in usurious times more important than honour
(8), and hence a link, via contrast, between buying votive candles
and swallowing one's honour to make two million. Usury makes us
leave beautiful ladies altogether, who coruscate through the suc-
cessions here, the "beauty of an ass cart" of XXX (1), Artemis
(2), Venus (3), Ignez (4-6), Madame Hyle (7). Abstractions also
undergo metamorphosis—Beauty, Pity, Time, Substance [Hyle],
Usury. Moreover, there is a movement traceable from visual perception (1) to invocation (2) to anecdote (3-5) back to visual
perception (6-7).

Each ideographic unit, by carrying so many connections, possesses
the sheer indecipherability of "L'Art 1910," even when ideas dominate it: because the ideas have their poetic function, *as distinct from
their signification*, only by juxtaposition to other ideas. We know
where Pound stands on pity and on usury, and what he thinks usury
has done to civilization, but not how these strongly held notions
relate to love or last things, to Odysseus or Pound (except by simple
negation). Usury is understood as clearly as the "Pine by the black
trunk of its shadow" is seen here; but its relationships in the poem
stand in obscure ideographic, aesthetic combination with other elements. So the visual scene of (1) can be broken down into several
smaller ideograms (a) glide, (b) lights and prow, (c) silver beaks,
(d) stone, (e) bough, (f) lamps, (g) pine, (h) hill, (i) trees. And
the more sensory the poem becomes, the harder its relations are to
grasp: the speaking poet moves to pure visual perception, which sets
a limit for his eyes just as pure quotation sets a limit for his thought;
both limits are moved up to and away from. His thought, his self-
definition, coruscates through the poem. The adaptations of the
diction tell us as much, from the persona-archaism of "Pity causeth
the forests" and the very spelling of "compleynt" to the harsh
"quoted" slang of "Honour, balls for yr. honour," and the abbrevi-
ated spelling of "yr." The visual precept of "imagism" can be incidental here; or central, as often in the *Pisan Cantos*. The personal
accent of the poet improvising an archaized "poetic" speech and the

ideographic set of a word "older" than those surrounding it, interact through the speaking person who is the history he projects.

He lives into that history he builds, living into history as the poem, and the life outside the poem, grow: the Pound of 1922 could never have dreamt of Pisa, and he is caught in the tragedy of the dream he did have, like the peasant who is taken, because he was doubtless actually seen by the writing Pound, to provide the beginning of the *Pisan Cantos*:

The enormous tragedy of the dream in the peasant's	
bent shoulders.	(1)
Manes! Manes was tanned and stuffed,	(2)
Thus Ben and la Clara *a Milano*	(3)
by the heels at Milano	
That maggots shd eat the dead bullock	(4)
DIGENES, *digenés*, but the twice crucified	
where in history will you find it?	(5)
yet say this to the Possum: a bang, not a whimper,	(6)
with a bang not with a whimper.	
To build the city of Dioce whose terraces are the	
colour of stars.	(7)
The suave eyes, quiet, not scornful	(8)
rain also is of the process.	(9)
What you depart from is not the way	(10)
and olive tree blown white in the wind	(11)
Washed in the Kiang and Han	
What whiteness will you add to this whiteness,	(12)
what candor?	

Here the units move with the speed of emotions that the actual sights stir on the prison-bared eyes, "out in the open." They move, too, with the great calm (*suave eyes, quiet*) of recapitulation; the question of form and substance, in life and embalmment, has been posed so repeatedly by now that Ignez does not have to be mentioned again for parallel with Manes. Malatesta can come out in the open and appear as Mussolini (3): Pound has come out in the open to correct, under cover of a nickname, his taciturn friend T. S. Eliot (5).

The ideograms build up, condense, and also expand in emotional effect. Because the person expands, his identity is to be found in the anonymity of an expanding series of ideographic units; they themselves are as cryptic as he; they are as imagistic, as spatially *there*, as he is temporally moving. There can be no end but the death of the writer to the person of this hero. No end, because his obscurity moves into the future of a life not yet come to term; it moves, too, into the very clarity of the blocs he offers as signatures for a self who can set out the full play of his ideas. That full play succeeds just because it must abide by changing rules, rules of relation between self and other, self and self, self and the seen, self and the word. Anonymity and identity are not fused: they keep changing off. We are enabled to come at them just for that reason. The book stays open.

Notes

1. Baudelaire, Charles, *Les Fleurs du Mal*, Paris (Pléiade), 1961, p.81.
2. Dickinson, Emily, *The Complete Poems*, Boston-Toronto, 1960, p.264.
3. Whitman, Walt, "Song of Myself," *Leaves of Grass*, New York, 1950, p.27.
4. Benn, Gottfried, *Gesammelte Gedichte*, Wiesbaden-Zurich, 1956, p.272.
5. Benn, *Probleme der Lyrik*, Wiesbaden, 1951, p.24.
6. *Gesammelte Gedichte*, p.202.
7. Ibid., p.35.
8. *Probleme der Lyrik*, p.6.
9. Williams, William Carlos, *The Selected Poems*, New York, 1949, p.110.
10. Montale, Eugenio, "Mediterraneo," *Ossi di Seppia*, Verona, 1956, p.71.
11. Ibid. p.45.
12. Reverdy, Paul, "Lueurs," *Main d'Oeuvre*, Paris, 1949, p.251.
13. Perse, St. John (pseud.) in *The Berkeley Review*, Berkeley, California, Winter, 1956, p.36.
14. Baudelaire, "Correspondances," *Les Fleurs du Mal*, p.11.
15. Rilke, Rainer Maria, "Die Sonette an Orpheus," II-29, *Sämtliche Werke*, Vol. I, Wiesbaden, 1955, p.770.
16. Strawson, P. F., *Individuals*, New York, 1963, pp. 168-220.
17. Rilke, op. cit., I-5, p.733.
18. Ibid., I-26, p.748.
19. *Leaves of Grass*, p.23.
20. "A Clean, Well-lighted Place," *The Short Stories of Ernest Hemingway*, New York, 1935, p.477.
21. Merleau-Ponty, Maurice, *Signes*, Paris, 1961, p.96.
22. Montale, Eugenio, *La Bufera*, Verona, 1957, p.11.
23. Moore, Marianne, *Collected Poems*, New York, 1951, p.16.
24. Ibid., p.56.
25. Ponge, Francis, *Le Parti Pris des Choses*, Paris, 1942, p.18.

26. Ponge, "L'Araignée," *Botteghe Oscure*, III, Rome, 1949, p.353.

27. *Poems of Gerard Manley Hopkins*, New York-London, 1948, p.74.

28. Ibid., p.73.

29. McLuhan, Herbert Marshall, "The Analogical Mirrors," *Gerard Manley Hopkins, By the Kenyon Critics*, Norfolk, Conn., 1945, pp. 15-27.

30. Reverdy, P., quoted in *L'Art Poetique*, Paris, 1956, p.497.

31. Pasternak, Boris, *Selected Writings*, New York, 1958, p.31.

32. Ibid., p.265.

33. *The Collected Poems of William Butler Yeats*, New York, 1956, p.211.

34. Mallarmé, Stéphane, *Oeuvres Complètes*, Paris, 1945, p.37.

35. Ibid., p.75.

36. Eliot, T. S., "Burnt Norton," *Four Quartets*, New York, 1943, p.4.

37. Mauron, Charles, commentary in *The Poems of Mallarmé*, New York, 1951, p.279.

38. Proust, Marcel, *À la Recherche du temps perdu*, Paris, 1954, III, p.456.

39. Mallarmé, op. cit., p.368.

40. Ibid., p.368.

41. Ibid., p.54.

42. Breton, Andre, "Tiki," in *Mid-Century French Poets*, ed. by Wallace Fowlie, New York, 1955, p.168.

43. Crane, Hart, "Atlantis," *The Collected Poems*, New York, 1933, p.57.

44. Quoted in *Dylan Thomas, Dog Among the Fairies*, by Henry Treece, London, 1956, p.37.

45. Thomas, Dylan, *The Collected Poems*, New York, 1953, p.109.

46. Merleau-Ponty, *Signes*, p.112.

47. Beckett, Samuel, *Malloy*, New York, 1955, p.8.

48. Ibid., p.38.

49. Ibid., p.88.

50. Ibid., p.17.

51. Empson, William, *Seven Types of Ambiguity*, London, 1949.

52. Pope, Alexander, *The Dunciad*, IV, 11. 201-2.

53. Lowell, Robert, *Life Studies*, London, 1959, p.17.

54. Swift, Jonathan, "The Battle of the Books," in *Gulliver's Travels and Other Writings*, New York, 1960?, p.377.

55. Kraus, Karl, *Die Dritte Walpurgisnacht*, München, 1952, p.17.
56. Pound, Ezra, *Personae*, New York, 1926, p.119.
57. Davie, Donald, *Articulate Energy*, London, 1955, p.156.
58. Perse, St. John, *Seamarks*, New York, 1958, p.4.
59. Ibid., p.8.
60. Rimbaud, Arthur, *Oeuvres*, Paris, 1952, p.189.
61. Ibid., p.182.
62. Trakl, Georg, *Die Dichtungen*, Salzburg, 1938, p.85.
63. Ibid., p.87.
64. Ibid., p.88.
65. Ibid., p.167.
66. Ibid., p.147.
67. Heidegger, Martin, *Unterwegs Zur Sprache*, Tübingen, 1959, p.43.
68. Ibid., p.21.
69. Rilke, *Sämtliche Werke*, I, p.718.
70. Trakl, *Die Dichtungen*, p.142.
71. Valéry, Paul, *Oeuvres*, Paris, 1960, Vol. I, p.641.
72. Ibid., p.96.
73. Char, René, *Hypnos Waking*, New York, 1956, p.32.
74. Ibid., p.8.
75. Ibid., p.52.
76. Ibid., p.184.
77. Stein, Arnold, "Structures of Sound in Donne's Verse," *The Kenyon Review*, Gambier, Ohio, Winter and Spring, 1951.
78. Valéry, *Oeuvres*, I, p.480.
79. Maritain, Jacques, *Creative Intuition in Art and Poetry*, New York, 1955, p.221.
80. Williams, William Carlos, *Pictures from Brueghel and Other Poems*, New York, 1962, p.35.
81. Montale, Eugenio, *Le Occasioni*, Verona 1954, p.29.
82. I have borrowed these terms from S. R. Levin, *Syntactic Structures in Poetry*, The Hague, 1961.
83. Lowell, Robert, "My Last Afternoon with Uncle Devereux Winslow," *Life Studies*, p.33.
84. Beloof, Robert, "Prosody and Tone: The 'Mathematics' of Marianne Moore," *The Kenyon Review*, Gambier, Ohio, Vol. XX, No 1, Winter 1958, pp.116-123.
85. Creeley, Robert, *For Love*, New York, 1962, p.91.

86. This is defined in an unpublished thesis on Wallace Stevens by Mac Hammond, (Harvard, 1963).

87. Moore, Marianne, *Collected Poems*, p.114.

88. Ibid., p.56.

89. *The Letters of Ezra Pound, 1907-1941*, ed. by D. D. Paige, New New York, 1950, "155: to Marianne Moore," p.142.

90. Crane, Hart, "Praise for an Urn," *The Collected Poems*, p.68.

91. Pound, *Personae*, p.204.

92. Berryman, John, "The Poetry of Ezra Pound," *Partisan Review*, New York, April, 1949, p.377-94.

93. Kenner, Hugh, "Under the Larches of Paradise," *Gnomon*, New York, 1958, p.280.

94. Pound, Ezra, *The Cantos*, New York, 1948, "XXIX," p.145.

95. Ibid., p.147.

96. Ibid., p.149.

97. Hough, Graham, *A Preface to The Faerie Queene*, New York, 1962, pp.100ff.

98. Fletcher, Angus, *Allegory*, Ithaca, New York, 1964.

99. Chaucer, *Romaunt of the Rose*, 11. 3031-3035.

100. Beckett, *Endgame, A Play in One Act*, New York, 1958, p.1.

101. Ibid., p.2.

102. Holland, Norman N., "Film, Metafilm, and Un-Film," *The Hudson Review*, Vol. XV, No. 3, Autumn 1962, p.406.

103. Beckett, *Waiting For Godot*, New York, 1954, p.61.

104. Freud, Sigmund, *Die Traumdeutung*, [1899], Vienna, 1950, p.214.

105. Ibid., p.210.

106. Kafka, Franz, *Hochzeitsvorbereitungen*, "Betrachtungen über Sünde Leid, Hoffnung, and den Wahren Weg," New York, 1953, p.49, No. 86.

107. Kafka, *Erzählungen*, New York, 1946, p.44.

108. Bense, Max, *Die Theorie Kafkas*, Köln-Berlin, 1952, p.33.

109. Kafka, *Der Prozess*, Berlin, 1953, pp.69-70.

110. Ibid., p.255.

111. Ibid., p.264.

112. Blanchot, Maurice, *L'Espace Littéraire*, Paris, 1955.

113. Kafka, *Tagebücher*, New York, 1954, p.568 (30 January 1922).

114. Emrich, Wilhelm, *Franz Kafka*, Bonn, 1958.

115. *Hochzeitsvorbereitungen*, p.48, No. 84.

116. Ibid., p.96.

117. Ibid., p.42, No. 26.
118. Ibid., p.50, No. 87.
119. Ibid., p.51, No. 97.
120. Ibid., p.51, No. 96.
121. Golding, William, *Lord of the Flies*, New York, 1959, p.186.
122. Golding, *The Inheritors*, London, 1961, p.233.
123. *Lord of the Flies*, p.127.
124. *The Inheritors*, p.43.
125. Golding, *Free Fall*, New York, 1959, p.196.
126. Ibid., p.186.
127. Ibid., p.5.
128. Bradbrook, M. C., *Themes and Conventions of Elizabethan Tragedy* [1935], London, 1960, pp.20-21.
129. Heywood, Thomas, *A Woman Killed with Kindness*, I, vi, 108–115, in *Elizabethan and Stuart Plays*, New York, 1934, p.653.
130. Ibid., I, vi, 142-145, p.653-54.
131. Ibid., I, vi, 154-165, p.654.
132. Shakespeare, *Pericles*, V, i, 107-114.
133. Ibsen, Henrik, *The Wild Duck*, in *Four Great Plays of Ibsen*, New York, 1959, p.219.
134. Ibid., pp.288-89.
135. Ibsen, *Ghosts*, op. cit., p.126.
136. *Four Great Plays by Chekhov*, New York, 1958, pp.58-59.
137. Chekhov, *The Cherry Orchard*, op. cit., p.91.
138. *Waiting for Godot*, p.7 (b).
139. Ionesco, Eugène, *Les Chaises*, in *Theâtre*, Paris, 1954, p.140.
140. Heidegger, *Sein und Zeit*, [1927] Tübingen, 1963, p.130.
141. Schlegel, F., *Schriften und Fragmente*, [1802] Stuttgart, 1956, p.132.
142. Rimbaud, letter to Georges Izambard, as quoted in *L'Art Poétique*, p.351.
143. Valéry, "Réflections simples sur le corps," *Oeuvres*, I, pp.923-30.
144. Ibid., p.130.
145. Yeats, *Collected Poems*, New York, 1956, p.232.
146. Valéry, op. cit., p.1613.
147. LaForgue, Jules, "Complainte de Lord Pierrot," *Oeuvres Complètes*, Paris, 1951, Vol. I, p.132.
148. Ibid., Vol. II, p.8.
149. Ibid., Vol. I, p.233.
150. Ibid., Vol. II, p.167.

151. Ibid., p.170.

152. Pasternak, *Selected Writings*, p.113.

153. Apollinaire, *Oeuvres Poétiques*, Paris, 1956, p.171.

154. Ibid., p.174.

155. Ibid., p.172.

156. Ibid., p.171.

157. Ibid., p.77.

158. Ibid., p.74.

159. *Life Studies*, p.31.

160. Char, *Hypnos Waking*, p.212.

161. *Gaudier-Brzeska*, [1916], New York, 1960, pp.94-106, as cited in Ellmann and Feidelson, *The Modern Tradition*, New York, 1965.

162. Pound, *Personae*, p.157.

163. Ibid., p.109.

164. Ibid., p.113.

165. Pound, "The Serious Artist," *Literary Essays*, London, 1954, p.50.

166. *The Cantos*, pp.146ff.

167. Pound, *The Spirit of Romance* [1910], New York, n.d., p.218.

Index

195

INDEX